P9-CCA-667

ALSO BY BILL SHORE

The Cathedral Within

Revolution of the Heart

THE LIGHT OF CONSCIENCE

THE LIGHT OF CONSCIENCE

How a Simple Act Can Change Your Life

BILL SHORE

RANDOM HOUSE TRADE PAPERBACKS
NEW YORK

2005 Random House Trade Paperback Edition

Published in the United States by Random House Trade Paperbacks, an imprint of The Random House Publishing Group, a division of Random House, Inc., New York.

RANDOM HOUSE TRADE PAPERBACKS and colophon are trademarks of Random House, Inc.

Originally published in hardcover in the United States by Random House, an imprint of The Random House Publishing Group, a division of Random House, Inc., in 2004.

Grateful acknowledgment is made to the following for permission to reprint previously published material:

Harcourt, Inc.: "In Praise of Feeling Bad About Yourself" from *View with a Grain of Sand* by Wisława Szymborska, copyright © 1993 by Wisława Szymborska. English translation by Stanisław Barańczak and Clare Cavanagh, copyright © 1995 by Harcourt, Inc. Reprinted by permission.

John Wiley & Sons, Inc.: Excerpt from "Leadership and the Inner Journey" by Parker J. Palmer from *Leader to Leader,* Fall 2001, no. 22, pages 26–33, copyright © 2001 Parker J. Palmer. Reprinted by permission of John Wiley & Sons, Inc.

Library of Congress Cataloging-in-Publication Data

Shore, William H.
The light of conscience : how a simple act can change your life / by Bill Shore.
p. cm.
ISBN 0-8129-7363-1
1. Conscience. I. Title.

BJ1471.S56 2004
170'.44—dc21 2003057066

Printed in the United States of America
www.atrandom.com

2 4 6 8 9 7 5 3 1

Book design by JoAnne Metsch

For Zach and Mollie,

and

Sofie

The buzzard never says it is to blame.
The panther wouldn't know what scruples mean.
When the piranha strikes, it feels no shame.
If snakes had hands, they'd claim their hands were clean.

A jackal doesn't understand remorse.
Lions and lice don't waver in their course.
Why should they, when they know they're right?

Though hearts of killer whales may weigh a ton,
in every other way they're light.

On this third planet from the sun
among the signs of bestiality
a clear conscience is Number One.

—Wisława Szymborska,

"In Praise of Feeling Bad About Yourself"

CONTENTS

I *Acts of Conscience Change the World* 3

II *Children and Conscience* 30

III *Conscience Sets the Agenda* 60

IV *Acts of Conscience Occur Every Day and All Around Us* 83

V *The Conscience of Moral Entrepreneurs* 141

VI *The Conscience of Leaders* 174

VII *The Art of Conscience* 192

VIII *Conscience Is Global* 212

IX *Conscience Is a Lighthouse* 242

Acknowledgments 267

THE LIGHT OF CONSCIENCE

I

Acts of Conscience Change the World

We must pass through solitude and difficulty, isolation and silence, to find that enchanted place where we can dance our clumsy dance and sing our sorrowful song. But in that dance, and in that song, the most ancient rites of conscience fulfill themselves in the awareness of being human.

—PABLO NERUDA,
Nobel lecture, December 13, 1971

SHIFTING SANDS

ON GOOSE ROCKS BEACH, a father dozes, baking in the sun, unsuspecting. He sprawls across a flat chaise longue, one hand hanging off but clutching a newspaper. His wife, on a beach chair next to him, reads while their three toddlers play at water's edge. A floppy hat shields her face from the heat.

They look to be in their late thirties, and judging by their young kids, they've probably been married just over ten years. They are an attractive couple, either comfortable with the silence between them or resigned to it. Odds are he works outside of Boston. Goose Rocks is not well known enough to attract people from afar. This is his week to get a tan, overeat, nap in the afternoon. Whatever stresses had to be incurred to get here, to afford this respite, whatever strains may have frayed bonds of family or marriage during the rest of the year, they are forgotten now. Almost.

Down by the water both girls are working the sand with shovels and rakes. The son, about four, uses a bucket for a more ambitious construction project. His name, Carl, has been shouted several times. The water is frigid and all three children keep an eye on it to avoid the surprise of a cold splash. Their mom, about twenty-five yards away, doesn't turn a page without checking on them. The waves are gentle, but just a few feet into the water there can be steep and sudden drop-offs. This worry is exclusively Mom's. Dad moves not a muscle. His chest rises and falls in gentle slumber. A family has achieved equilibrium. Almost.

The boy and his bucket edge closer to the water, but when he feels the icy darts nip at his feet he retreats, catches his breath, charges, and retreats again. His mother pays closer attention but doesn't abandon her book. Carl must hold all of the family's excess energy like a reservoir, and while he spins and twirls, charges and retreats, and finds himself acclimating to the colder temperatures, he turns and faces the part of the beach where he remembers having left his parents. Mom's nose is in the book. Dad dreams.

Carl has an idea. Carl edges a little deeper into the water. He runs and slips, but a fall is not a fall at that age, just the prelude to a bounce. His body twists in a shiver. He uncoils and then lowers the yellow bucket down to fill it up full. He looks back toward his parents. The idea is a mission now. He walks up the sand as quickly as he can without spilling any of the cold ocean he has captured. His white tummy juts out ahead of him. He calls "Daddy" but he is too far away and Daddy is no more conscious than the seaweed strewn across the sand.

When he reaches his father, Carl pulls the bucket back with both arms and makes the motion of dumping the water on his dad. Only he's not looking in that direction, but instead at his mom. It's a solicitation of sorts, a long-shot appeal up the chain of command. Mom puts one hand over her mouth to suppress a giggle. Carl, bucket poised, looks over at Dad and then at Mom again. Dad snores on. Mom's eyes dance. Permission granted.

Carl cannot believe his good luck. He steps up closer on a mound of sand, goes through the motions again, and balks. He is giving his mother one last chance, as if he intuitively understands there is a larger dynamic at work.

Mom all but freezes, careful now, unprepared to step further past the line she has already crossed. Carl correctly takes silence as assent and hurls the icy water on top of his sleeping father.

"My God!" The father jumps out of the chaise longue as if

jabbed by an electric cattle prod. He screams in shock and agony, and his head rolls around on his neck as if searching to see the snake that may strike again before the snake sees him. Calming, he shakes himself like a poodle that didn't like its shampoo. When he sees Carl standing in front of him with the empty bucket, he is disbelieving. When he realizes his wife has been sitting next to him the entire time, he is not only disbelieving but furious.

"Did you see that he was going to do that?" he shouts incredulously. His jaw juts and the rest of his body leans in the same direction, both hands hanging down at his sides.

His wife bears no trace of the mischievous giggle now. Her eyes open wide to show her surprise. She is on the verge of taking offense at being unjustly accused. It is what Siskel and Ebert used to call Oscar-worthy.

"No. Of course not."

Her husband surveys the scene and glares, defeated by the absence of a smoking gun. He will have to accept whatever truce is eventually proffered. Awake only moments, he finds himself at stalemate.

"I swear I didn't," she protests.

From my spot on the beach a few yards away it's hard to ascertain malice. I doubt she woke up this morning planning this. More likely she made a bad choice in a split second, regretting it even before the water left the bucket. Now she is too flustered or insecure to own up to it and takes refuge in the lack of fingerprints.

Maybe all of this is a complete aberration. Every family has moments when the window shade snaps up at the wrong time, revealing what is their business and theirs alone. Outsiders interpret at their own peril. But it seems the sands have shifted under all three of them. The water by itself, no matter how cold, creates no permanent harm. But even the smallest deception makes the road to the next one that much smoother. Mom has her guilt, Dad has his doubts, and Carl knows something about the two of them that he doesn't really want to know. There is no longer an unbroken line between Carl and his parents, but a triangle instead.

Carl and his family still have half a week left of their vacation. The gentleness of Goose Rocks Beach will surely reassert itself. The tides will come and go on schedule. The waves will never cease. The sun will shine just as brightly tomorrow. Almost.

EVERYONE SEEKS CHANGE

I HAVE COME to a place you've probably never heard of to write about how acts of conscience can change the world.

It is a place called Goose Rocks Beach.

America has 88,363 miles of tidal shoreline. This remote and rocky little stretch in down-east Maine comprises three of them.

I don't think it is an accident that I chose this place, or an accident that I decided to write about acts of conscience after years of experiencing nature's reassuring rhythms amid such quiet and isolation. One's inner voice is easier to hear in the stillness here than in any place I've ever been.

Changing the world has been a lifelong ambition of mine. I am almost embarrassed by how immodest and foolhardy that sounds. But I am not alone. Changing the world may not be an ambition everyone shares, but the differences between people on this are of degree more than of principle.

Almost everyone seeks change in some way large or small. We want better schools for our children, safer streets, and cleaner parks. We work out to change our weight or shape. We make New Year's resolutions, read best-selling how-to books, watch Oprah and Dr. Phil. We vote, volunteer, and contribute to charity. We write op-eds and letters to the editor. Mothers organize against drunk driving. Neighbors lobby for quieter airports. We create art. We pray for peace. In countless other ways unique to our species, we are driven to create change. The longer and harder we pursue it, the more important it becomes to understand where it begins, what precipitates it, and what kind of actions can be leveraged to greatest consequence.

When it comes to creating change, I've pursued many and varied avenues: government service, presidential politics, business, philanthropy, humanitarian aid, social entrepreneurship, and even writing books.

I worked for two United States senators, both Democrats and both unsuccessful candidates for president. I started a nonprofit antihunger organization, Share Our Strength, which has grown to be one of the largest in the nation. For nearly two decades, I helped build other community service organizations, like City Year, which President Clinton used as a model for AmeriCorps, and the Echoing Green Foundation. I launched a for-profit consulting firm, Community Wealth Ventures, to help nonprofits be more sustainable by creating their own wealth instead of redistributing the wealth of others. I've taught at universities and business schools. And I've traveled the globe to assess the needs of children, whether they are victims of famine in Africa or of malnutrition in the United States, granting funds to build food banks, dig wells, staff hospitals, and support advocacy.

Each avenue afforded the opportunity to make vital contributions. But each also had its limitations. As the clock ticked and the years passed, as the reality of finite time and money grew clearer, I felt an ever-growing desire to identify and understand the means of leveraging the greatest change—not incremental or evolutionary but catalytic change that could inspire and move millions and could address problems on the scale on which they exist. Problems like hunger, poverty, and illiteracy that were not going to yield to the solutions that came from charity or even government.

The more I thought about those we associate with sweeping change—Gandhi, Dr. Martin Luther King, Jr., Rosa Parks, Jackie Robinson—the more I realized the central role that acts of conscience played in their achievements. They derived their power not from political office or great wealth but from their willingness to abide their own conscience, even when they were in the minority.

We tend to think that creating change requires an array of external resources and support: acts of Congress, great sums of money, large standing armies, technology, vast research capabilities, or powerful lobbyists, relationships, and networks. And of course they all have their place. But often the most sweeping change results from a single individual with none of those at his or her command but, instead, with the courage to follow his or her conscience. When Gandhi said, "You must become the change you wish to see in the world," he acknowledged conscience as the great equalizer. We all have the same ability and the same responsibility to bring about change.

Arthur Miller, in discussing why he wrote *The Crucible,* his play about the Salem witch trials that was an allegory for the McCarthy era, explained that based on his study of history, "It occurred to me that as improbable as it might seem, there were moments when an individual conscience was all that could keep a world from falling."

This is a book of stories about such moments. They are not essays with a pronounced point of view or op-ed columns reflecting a certain ideological embrace. Rather, they are stories in the old-fashioned sense, about mostly ordinary people who were capable of having an extraordinary impact when they found themselves in situations they neither sought nor asked for. The people in these stories run the gamut from washerwomen to military heroes, from sports champions to artists of all kinds, all of whom have only one element in common, the call of conscience. They are presented for the reader to experience in his or her own way: whether you are provoked, challenged, entertained, or inspired, the stories are here to draw your own lessons from, not mine. Conscience, by definition, is personal. A choice that is a no-brainer to one may be another's moral quandary. The meaning of each story that follows is something only you can decide.

MOMENTS YOU DON'T GET BACK

EVERY LIFE INCLUDES pivotal moments, roads taken or not, choices made on reflex rather than reflection. What makes such circumstances pivotal is that although their consequences may be long-lasting or even permanent, their specifics can't be anticipated or prepared for. Your reaction can't be scripted or calculated in advance. The choices you make depend upon and reveal your true character, both at the same time. Former U.S. senator Bob Kerrey, referring to a horrific personal experience during Vietnam on a night innocent women and children were mistakenly killed, describes these as "the moments you don't get back."

We all struggle at times to know what to do to seek and abide our conscience—when right and wrong are not black and white, when heart and head speak with different voices, when our intentions and our interests are not aligned. If you believe that the outcome of these struggles affects the course of your life, and the lives around you, then this book is for you.

If you believe that there are times and places when the choice an individual makes to speak or be silent, to eat or fast, to remain seated or to stand up in a crowd, to stare and remember or to walk on by and forget, can be as powerful as a president's command, a congressional appropriation, or a military incursion, then this book is for you.

This book is for you if your profession is rewarding financially but not spiritually, or if you've ever worried that your career and your conscience conflict.

This book is for you if you are a parent, hopeful your children will grow up to do the right thing even if no one is watching.

This book is for you if you question whether the countless small decisions and choices you make each day add up to a larger judgment about your life's meaning.

Finally, this book is for you if you believe that quiet, often solitary acts of conscience have echoes louder than the original sound; that individual acts have the potential to trigger large public consequences and continue to inspire others from generation to generation; that such acts bring rewards to the individual, that unforeseen benefits accrue, that one gains more than was sacrificed, and that there is a transformative power and richness to a life so lived.

Such acts of conscience are often, though not always, separate and distinct from public leadership or the calculated decisions, however courageous, of presidents and prime ministers. They cut across all walks of life—sports, business, family, religion, art, public affairs—and are performed by ordinary people who rise to occasions in extraordinary ways. They reinforce the fundamental premise of Share Our Strength and so many other community-serving organizations: that one person can make a difference.

This belief is the essential precursor to every act of philanthropy and advocacy, to writing a check or to extending a helping hand. It is the faith upon which all social change is conceived, the bedrock of every effort to serve country and community. It is what keeps a soldier in his platoon and a Peace Corps volunteer in her village when the odds of success or even survival seem slim. It is the impulse that holds the doctor to the O.R. and the teacher to the classroom. It is the essence of the American character.

We want to believe we can make a difference. Seeing and knowing how others have done so reinforces and validates that impulse. The themes attached to conscience are universal. Each of us has the ability, and ultimately the need, to live a life of conscience. We strive to instill it in our children. Businesses are increasingly learning that it is profitable. Contrary to expectations, it yields more benefit than cost. This is what John Kennedy acknowledged in his inaugural address nearly half a century ago when he challenged Americans to ask what they could do for their country, and promised "a good conscience our only sure reward."

THE STILL SMALL VOICE WITHIN

GOOSE ROCKS BEACH hides in plain view. It sits at the tip of the continent, connected to the coastal road by a soggy thread of marshland, and far enough away to be self-contained. There are no shops or restaurants here, just four hundred homes scattered about a double horseshoe curve, and a general store open eight weeks a year.

If you've ever wrestled with your conscience, Goose Rocks Beach is one place you are certain to get pinned to the mat. If one's conscience had an echo chamber, it would be located in a place like this. If you don't know your own mind here, you won't know it anywhere. You can stay with a thought. A thought can stay with you. There are no meetings, horns, radios, cars, e-mails, stores, planes, or cell phones to bump it aside. They exist, of course, but they are unnecessary here.

Truths cannot be avoided. This is a spot where the world dwarfs you—the land under your feet, the endless sea in front of you—but, paradoxically, you're at the center of it. Somehow, standing at the very edge of a great continent, you find your balance. When no longer in motion, you can travel the furthest toward your self.

This has long been a central tenet of the philosophy of the Quakers. Robert Lawrence Smith is the former headmaster of Sidwell Friends School in Washington, D.C., the country's largest Quaker day school. In *A Quaker Book of Wisdom,* he writes:

> Quakers believe that only when we have silenced our voices and our souls can we hear "the still small voice" that dwells within each of us—the voice of God that speaks to us and that we express to others through our deeds. Only by listening in stillness for that voice and letting it guide our actions can we truly let our lives speak.
>
> The cultivated ability to hear that voice is the most enduring value of silence. If we can locate, at the very center of silence, our individual "still small voice," we will have found our greatest ally in life. Because if we listen to that voice with an open heart, it will guide us through the most challenging crossroads of our lives: in work, in love, in distinguishing right from wrong.

Solitude and reflection are greater gifts than sun and sand. As prerequisites to bringing about change, they are mighty tools. History is instructive. Leaders of the greatest mass movements are often those who have also spent the greatest amount of time alone. Mandela, Gandhi, King. Aung San Suu Kyi in Burma. Sometimes it was jail or house arrest. Sometimes prayer. Sometimes fasting. Each used an intuitive understanding of solitude to a purpose.

The vital ingredients of social change are often thought to be funding, grassroots organizing, entrepreneurship, passion, innovation, idealism, and charismatic leadership. All play important roles. But first come solitude and reflection. They are what enables the foundation to set and solidify.

Thomas Merton, who lived an often solitary existence as a Trappist monk, wrote, "What is said here about solitude is not just a recipe for hermits. It has a bearing on the whole future of man and his world. . . . To be a person implies responsibility and freedom, and both these imply a certain interior solitude, a sense of personal integrity, a sense of one's own reality and one's ability to give himself to society—or to refuse that gift."

Goose Rocks is one of those places quiet enough outside to get quiet inside, to hear the inner voice as trustworthy as it is deep. You can reflect about what you'd like your life to look like, what is important to you, and what is important to be true to. As former Quaker headmaster Smith concluded: "Friends view silence as a highly accessible treasure: its benefits are unquestioned. The riches that silence offers are available to any one at any age and in any place. . . . The key ingredient is not so much the absence of noise as receptivity and access to the 'still small voice within.' "

For so many the attraction of a place like Goose Rocks is the ocean and its recreations. For me it is silence. Never is that more pronounced than late at night or in the early hours before dawn, when I stand at the picture window and gaze at the ocean. One night I noticed on the horizon across the water a brief twinkling of light. I tried to ascertain if it was a boat, a house, or an island, and then I realized it must be a lighthouse somewhere on the coast.

The light's flash was so low on the horizon and so quick that it was hard to find again just a moment later. It's amazing to contemplate the light's power. From where I stood it was no more than a pinpoint or the flash of a firefly. Yet paying attention to its flicker could be the difference between success and failure, between life and death. Even when Goose Rocks was at its most deserted, it was a reminder that one is never completely alone. I made up my mind to find the source of the light, to seek it out, to inquire and to explore its origins.

A PERSONAL JOURNEY

WHILE GROWING UP in the 1960s, during the Vietnam War and the civil rights era, I watched people try to effect change through civil disobedience, rallies, and protest marches, by answering John F. Kennedy's call to public service, or by joining Lyndon Johnson's war on poverty. The goals were often to create government institutions, like the Peace Corps, much as FDR did during the New Deal, agencies whose services would create change.

The changing-the-world industry was at one time headquartered in government, but idealists weren't satisfied there for long. Vietnam and Watergate precipitated a diminished confidence in government and politics as a source of change. Like the steelmakers who fled my hometown, Pittsburgh, seeking higher productivity elsewhere, many activists sought alternative venues.

Also as government and politics became increasingly sophisticated and specialized, they also became more elitist and exclusive. In an essay about the 1988 presidential campaign called "Insider Baseball," Joan Didion wrote that politics had become "a mechanism seen as so specialized that access to it is correctly limited to its own professionals, to those who manage policy and those who report on it, to those who run the polls and those who quote them, to those who ask and those who answer the questions on the Sunday shows, to the media consultants, to the columnists, to the issues advisers, to those who give the off-the-record breakfasts and those who attend them; to that handful of insiders who invent, year in and year out, the narrative of public life."

After the Kennedy assassinations, Vietnam, and Watergate, government institutions lost their luster. Dynamic individuals led protest movements and tore down racist institutions, and then when the time came to build new ones, it was left to social entrepreneurs, who, instead of going into government or leading protests, began to create and build powerful community-based civic organizations.

Today's agents of change are often individual entrepreneurs. Business entrepreneurs have redefined our economy. Our civic institutions have been refashioned by social entrepreneurs. Perhaps most important of all, moral entrepreneurs have introduced a new moral dimension into industries, professions, communities, and society. The same committed conscience that led one generation into government and another to oppose it now devotes itself to building positive alternatives bridging the private and public sectors.

Acts of conscience often originate with a single person, but their power is in motivating larger numbers of individuals to act. Efforts to change the world are often hindered by constraints of time, talent, resources, even imagination. Acts of conscience can overcome them all.

I initially thought acts of conscience were mostly political in nature, and rare, and that like exotic birds I might get a glimpse of them if I searched long and stared hard enough. I wanted to collect as many as possible and describe their features for others. I found instead that they are ubiquitous. They are not confined to political affairs or legendary leaders. They do not revolve only around people featured in history books. They can be found in religion, business, sports, art, and every other field of human endeavor. Acts of conscience are as much the province of laundry workers, photographers, jockeys, and painters as of presidents and popes. What is rare is a day whose national and local news doesn't turn on some issue of conscience. I thought the task would require the equivalent of a microscope to dissect and study what I assumed was hard to find and see. What I really needed was a telescope to reveal the dazzling array of stars that surrounds us.

At first I saw acts of conscience as something separate from the familiar panoply of activities that create change: legislation, political leadership, philanthropy, community-based activism, and community wealth creation. But I realized they are the essential precursors, that is, they are what precipitates each of the efforts listed above, what creates both the energy and the climate for achieving change. There is no way to separate acts of conscience from the ongoing effort to improve the social conditions in which people live. Social change is uncertain, hardscrabble work. To the extent it grows from the mixed soil of concern, compassion, and courage to act, acts of conscience are the water that brings it to life.

Finally, I believed that the lessons to be mined from acts of conscience were timeless and, like morality, were fixed points, anchored in values that do not change. While that may be true, their application is constantly changing, and indeed what keeps acts of conscience alive and relevant is the moral entrepreneurs who introduce conscience-based moralities into new environments, industries, communities, and professions, whether that be entertainment, hospitality, or high tech. If it weren't for moral entrepreneurs creating modern-day applications, the principles of conscience would be relegated to history books and Bibles. There would be no bridge between their being taught and their being lived.

At the center of any exploration of conscience, at the heart of it, is a deeply personal journey. It is a journey that can be mapped only by listening to your own inner voice above and beyond those of others, by staying true to something that at its core is called *self*. This book reflects, records, and profiles the journeys many have taken, though much of it is through the prism of my own. So if it reads in places as if based on my journals, my travels, what has moved or shocked me or opened my eyes, my quest to make my work more meaningful, and my experience of rearing children, that's because it is. If it seems that historic acts of national and international consequence are experienced alongside the more prosaic and mundane activities of daily living, it's because as we live life, they are. I selected and pursued those travels, readings, visits, art exhibits, and experiences for the different aspects of conscience they would reveal. When I recount them here, it is so that you can discover what I discovered. That is both the strength and the weakness of a quest that must be personal to be effective.

This is definitely not a how-to book. There are no 7 Habits or 10 Rules. In fact the central point of the book is just the opposite: that the most important voice to listen to is your own.

CONSCIENCE AND CALLING

ON A SPRING day in 2002, I took the train to Philadelphia to lecture at the Fox Leadership Program at the University of Pennsylvania. The series invites graduates to return and tell the students about the choices they made, obstacles they overcame, and what aspects of their education at Penn were the most valuable to them. The objective is to inspire, or at the very least to reassure students that their lives will not be the train wreck they envision, or, at least, that it is never too late to recover from whatever train wreck they may experience.

I rarely pass up an opportunity to speak to college students. So much depends on their seeing the field of community service as a career opportunity rather than a career detour. That kind of culture shift for nonprofits will literally take generations. Students are not an easy audience, but they are an honest one. If you're boring or they are tired they will yawn while you're speaking without ever breaking eye contact. They'll ask whatever is on their mind, with no filter. Many of their questions reflect clear notions about right and wrong that are destined to lose their clarity with age.

My lecture was in the Great Hall of a wonderful old ivy-covered building on Locust Walk, the main thoroughfare that runs from one end of Penn's campus to the other.

Though it was still February, the temperature neared sixty degrees. The day was so gorgeous I couldn't imagine who would attend. Students were strolling everywhere. A loud band had formed on the lawn, with the spontaneity that is such a distinguishing hallmark of student life. Near the library and college green, hundreds of students lounged on the grass, heads on backpacks, while others tossed Frisbees as they reveled in the first false spring of the season.

The beauty of Locust Walk this lovely day was marred only by flyers with my name on them taped to the ground every ten to fifteen yards, bearing the black scuff marks of shoes that had trodden obliviously over them. It seemed a desperate and dubious last resort at crowd building. Maybe it worked. To my surprise, enough students turned out to fill the Great Hall. Though it was a high-ceilinged room, I could speak without a microphone and still be heard over the band outside the open windows. I stood in front of the lectern, closer to the crowd, pouring extra energy into the thirty-minute talk. That energy and more came back to me from the students during the question-and-answer period.

"Do you really believe that if you follow your dream everything will turn out okay?" asked a young black woman standing in the back, both skeptical and hopeful in the same breath. Though I had said no such thing, I suppose I'd cloaked myself in the garment from which she'd pulled this thread.

"How do you define passion?" asked another.

"Is there a mantra you repeat or a philosophy you adhere to that gives you confidence to be creative and to be a leader?"

"How did Penn prepare you for what you're doing now?"

Their interests, reflected in their majors, were wildly diverse: urban planning, biology, sociology, environmental science, international development, psychology. But their questions all seemed to flow from the same headwaters. More than anything else they wanted to be reassured that their conscience and career choices weren't at odds with each other, that they could maintain their idealism and still get ahead. Many assume they will have to find a way to make their ideals square with the career they choose, rather than having the confidence that they can design a career consistent with their ideals.

A sophomore named Sarah e-mailed me the next day, explaining that whenever she confides her ambition to friends or family, the "reaction is always the same: You know there is no money in nonprofits. This is why when you stated that over the last twenty years the idea of choice of what to do after graduation has changed from being a decision about creating wealth or serving the public interest to a challenge to create wealth for public interest you made my day. . . . I was able to leave with a newfound confidence."

I tried to persuade them that the most reliable navigation tools are internal, not external, that they should pay attention to their deepest emotions and act on them rather than push them away as if they were inconvenient. Make your life's work about whatever makes you angry, outraged, thrilled, or fulfilled. Trust your conscience. Even if you are not always faithful to it, it will always be honest with you.

The students also shared a misconception that there is a special list of ingredients and that if someone would tell them what they are, and they could just get their hands on them and mix them together the right way, their lives would turn out as they wish. They assume that the only form success takes is an unbroken string. They're still a decade or two away from appreciating the value that can be extracted from the inevitable missteps, bad breaks, and stubborn charges up the wrong hill.

It seemed like a good time to remind them, notwithstanding how deftly I tend to skip over it, that I had been the key architect of three consecutive losing presidential campaigns. Some of them were just being born in the year I helped one candidate accumulate a four-million-dollar campaign debt that would never be repaid. Others were in preschool, three years later, during the campaign in which I sold my home, lost my job, was stranded for nine months two thousand miles from friends and family, and ended up with tear-stained cheeks on the front page of *The Washington Post*. And most were in elementary school when I capped this decade-long run in 1992, helping Bob Kerrey win a total of one primary.

The relief in the Great Hall was palpable. Conclusive proof of life after failure. I saw the realization beginning to dawn that detours on the road to success may make the journey longer, but they will also make it more scenic.

There are ventures to be launched that can be capitalized by conscience. Unlike some start-ups, such ventures don't need to be continuously recapitalized. With conscience as capital, when one draws down on the account its assets increase rather than dwindle. A generation's true potential may depend on their faith in this truth.

CONSCIENCE AND HOPE

EACH YEAR THE Baton Rouge Area Foundation sponsors the Marcia Kaplan Kantrow lecture, named for their first program officer, who died young from cancer. I didn't know her, but I'd read about her, and the foundation staff spoke with genuine emotion of her spirit and commitment to community. Her family gathers for this annual lecture, traveling from other parts of the state and from as far away as Chicago. On the night when I had been invited to deliver the annual address, I met her parents: her mother, whose white hair was set off by a regal purple dress, and her father, whose eyes beamed through large rimmed glasses. As they walked slowly arm in arm down the side aisle, leaning on and into each other, it was difficult to tell who was supporting whom. Also present were her brother, sister, daughter, and grandson.

The lecture is held on the Louisiana State University campus at the Lod Cook Alumni Center, with its floor-to-ceiling windows on one side affording a large arched view of the lake. The lectern stands on the floor, not on a stage, making it easy to come out from behind it and approach the audience. The standing-room-only crowd had less to do with my presence than with last year's catastrophe: fewer than twenty-five people showed up, and the organizer was fired on the spot. Whoever organized it this year wasn't taking any chances.

I don't know if you can teach old dogs new tricks, but old speakers can feel new emotions. I gave the speech I often give, about the need for nonprofits to create community wealth and about the ethic of cathedral building. I didn't say anything I hadn't said a hundred times before. I talked about how each of us has as great a role as our military in keeping America united and strong, about how nonprofits are worth more than they think they are. I described the success of nonprofits that have created wealth for themselves.

But despite saying what I always say, it was not an evening like any other. As I neared the end of my remarks and started to talk about the ancient cathedral builders who did not live to see their work finished, Marcia Kaplan Kantrow's parents came into focus in the first row. The central truth of the evening became obvious. A family had gathered, and a community had assembled, in memory of a woman they knew, not a distant mythic figure, but a real woman they loved and remembered for the way she labored with energy and passion yet who was denied the gratification of seeing the results of her efforts. Stepping from behind the lectern as I spoke, I took a few steps toward the first-row seats of Marcia Kantrow's parents, acknowledging her and gesturing toward them with outstretched hand.

Literary metaphor sprang to life. Without taking her eyes off me, the elderly Mrs. Kantrow reached over and gripped the forearm of her husband. It was a swift motion, synchronized to my words, charged with intimacy.

I don't pretend to understand for even one moment the swirl of emotions that engulf a parent who has buried a child, or the test of faith and search for meaning one endures. Five years or even five lifetimes might not be enough to come to terms with it. But I thought I saw in the grip of that mother's fingers on her husband's sleeve a fleeting respite of peace, a flicker of affirmation that Marcia's brief life and eternal aftermath made sense. It was something to clutch and not let go.

After the speech, Marcia's mother was one of many to walk up and thank me. But I was the grateful one. The Kantrow family had reminded me of something we too easily forget: People are strong. They can endure the unimaginable. They can persist beyond all reason. They can toil without resource or recognition. So long as they have hope. It need not be hope that they will prevail. Only that their efforts matter, that their caring will amount to something, that they can make a difference.

Of all we seek to impart to those we strive to serve—money, laws, grants, programs, policies, conferences, technical assistance—all are necessary and valuable, but hope alone is indispensable. Conscience is its cradle. It is where hope is nurtured and protected and grows. The hunger for hope is the greatest hunger of all.

II

Children and Conscience

The conscience is the voice within us that has really heard the voices of others (starting with our parents, of course) and so whispers and sometimes shouts oughts and naughts to us, guides us in our thinking and doing. The conscience constantly presses its moral weight on our feeling lives, our imaginative life. Without doubt, most elementary school children are not only capable of discerning between right and wrong, they are vastly interested in how to do so—it's a real passion for them.

—ROBERT COLES,
The Moral Intelligence of Children

WE WERE ALL THIRTEEN ONCE

"ZACH, I HAVE a question for you. What was the worst decision you made last night?"

We are sitting in my study, at least I am sitting, while my son stands stiffly, with all of the tension of trying too hard to look relaxed. It is his thirteenth birthday, and nine other teenage boys slept over last night. While they watched videos and *Saturday Night Live*, I worked in my study until past one o'clock. Zach checked in with me a couple of times, which I should have recognized as a warning sign. At about one-fifteen I told him I was going to sleep. I urged that they get to bed by two, but I wasn't optimistic and didn't really care. For some reason, raw parental instinct I suppose, I asked: "No one's going anywhere, right, Zach? I mean, no one leaves the house for any reason. Right?"

It seemed like a ludicrous question at that hour, and he shrugged it off with the casual air he thought it deserved. But I later realized he did not answer it directly.

To my surprise, I slept soundly. I never had to quiet the boys. It was as if they weren't even there. Hmmm . . .

When I looked in on them in the morning, they were fast asleep, sprawled across the floor like a load of logs spilled on a highway. I walked into the bathroom and noticed there was no toilet paper, which didn't surprise me given the number of houseguests. I went to the pantry, where a dozen rolls of toilet paper are usually stacked high. There were none. The night's tranquillity had been an illusion.

I got in the car and drove straight to the Witkins' house at the top of a hill three blocks away. Zach had had a minor run-in with them once over a dented mailbox. It was a good two years ago but it had involved his friend Joey, one of the boys sleeping over, and I knew neither of them had forgotten it.

The reliability of their memories did not disappoint. Two dozen ribbons of tattered white toilet paper were arched and tangled in the large tree that shades the Witkins' house. It also streamed up over their gutters and roof. Only a strong rain would bring it down, and none was forecast for days.

I waited until all of the boys left before calling Zach into my study. He seemed genuinely puzzled by my question, so I repeated it.

"What was the worst decision you made last night? Please answer carefully. I'm concerned not only about what you did, but about your answering honestly now." Standard rule of interrogation: never let 'em know how much you know.

"We didn't do anything, Dad."

"That's not what I asked."

"What do you mean?"

"I thought we agreed no one was leaving this house."

"No one did."

"Zach!"

"What?"

"I know you guys were outside this house." I still haven't said what else I know so he takes one more shot.

"Oh that. Yeah, we were on the back deck just for a little bit."

I see his mind racing as if solving simultaneous equations. No fingerprints on toilet paper. Nothing can be proved.

I soften my voice. "Zach, I know about the Witkins. And the toilet paper. I know every single thing you did last night."

His face falls in crushing disappointment. He is apprehensive about the fate that awaits him, but impressed at the same time. He doesn't ask but he's desperate to know how I know.

"I was thirteen once, Z. I know most of what you're going to think and do before you think and do it. There's almost nothing you could get into that I didn't get into at the same age. And on top of that, you're made from me."

"We didn't hurt anything, Dad," he says, falling back to a further line of retreat.

"I know that, son, but what you're going to have to do now is go up there and knock on their door and tell them it was you and your friends, and that you're sorry."

Now he looks stricken, as if there is not a bit of difference between knocking at the Witkins' door and climbing a flagpole naked.

"But, Dad, there's no way they could ever even know it was me."

"Yes, but I know. And more important, you do too."

"I can't do it, Dad," he says, almost pleadingly. He doesn't mean he's refusing to do it. He means he is literally not able to. I remember how terrifying it is to make such a confession to adult strangers, how larger than life and stern they can look. My parents made me do the same thing for calling our neighbor Sam Simon "Baldy."

"I'm going to do you one big favor, son," I offer, because I think it will genuinely help him. "I'm going to give you a little tip. You need to know you are going to knock on that door and apologize before the day is over. That's not even negotiable and I guarantee it is going to happen. The tip is this: You can wait till tonight and spend the day in misery dreading it, or you can get it over with in the next five minutes. Why don't you get in the car?"

To my amazement, he does. We pull up in front of their house and park by the tree that now looks more like a fireworks display. He looks at me as if to ask, "Is this enough, that I proved I was willing to do it?"

"It only counts if you actually do it, Z."

I watch him walk to the door and speak to Mr. Witkin, who doesn't cut him much slack. I ache for him, but I'm proud too, and pleased. It's been an inexpensive lesson but a valuable one.

THE SECRETS WE TELL

SEVERAL TIMES EVERY week, people tell me secrets about their children.

A professor at Duke University remembers standing in his front yard one spring evening smoking a cigarette and looking up at the stars when he noticed his son jumping out of the second story bedroom window after he thought his parents were asleep. A retired naval officer in San Diego's Rotary Club learned that his daughter was taking marijuana brownies to school. The father of a high school hockey player recalls answering the phone at two o'clock in the morning and, mistaken for his son, being asked in a hushed voice, "Where did you disappear to when the police showed up?" One mom whispered to me about her daughter's suspension from the cheerleading squad for sipping vodka before a football game. An education consultant in New York remembers the night her father had to go to the police station because all three of her brothers had been arrested.

You might think I know these people intimately, or that I am their therapist, social worker, or priest. Far from it. The confessions are unsolicited. They are offered by complete strangers. It is often the first and last conversation we will have, this exchange about what once worried or embarrassed them, which they now feel free to share.

I hear such stories because of the door I open when sharing details about the lives of my own teenage children. I do this often. Part of my job is to give speeches. I give more than one hundred a year, from keynote addresses to college commencements. After the antihunger work of Share Our Strength became more visibly successful, and especially after the publication of my first two books, I was frequently asked to address the annual conferences of various organizations and associations interested in making a difference in their community. Often my role on the agenda represents a well-intentioned but potentially awkward digression from the primary, PowerPoint-driven focus of their meetings, which typically dwell on operational issues ranging from increased use of bar codes for managing inventory to a briefing on how derivatives strengthen gross margins.

I've spoken to almost every kind of gathering imaginable: venture capitalists, law firms, nutritionists, hospital administrators, restaurant employees, Peace Corps volunteers, magazine publishers, sitcom stars, international development consultants, church congregations, and college students.

My name and work are unknown to virtually all of them except perhaps the chair of the speakers' committee who invited me. Most sit bleary-eyed from the previous evening's obligatory away-from-home revelry, politely flipping through their three-ring conference binders, thinking to themselves, "Why couldn't we get anyone famous to speak this year?"

Born of the ensuing desperation, my objectives are to establish a common bond with the audience, to relax them so that I can relax, by conveying that my presentation will be neither preachy nor painful. Audiences credit you with being thoughtful if you are funny, but with being boring if you are too thoughtful. So the goal is a rhythmic balance of the two. As Warren Beatty told *The New York Times* when asked why he chose to make the movie *Bulworth* to get across a serious message: "If it's not entertaining, its just C-SPAN."

Given the diverse nature of the audiences I address, it's unlikely I'd have much in common with them all, except possibly that we have kids. Worst case, I can assume we were all kids once. So that is where I begin most speeches and often how I close. A talk about corporate responsibility, or ethics, or world hunger, or national service, starts with a story about Zach and Mollie. It might be their first high school dance. Or the time I lent Zach my car and he used it to shuttle half his senior class to the mall after first period. Or the time I received a letter from the principal that began, "On Friday, your child made the unfortunate choice to . . ."

I don't showcase these adventures based on any fantasy that my children possess gifts so special as to justify parental boasting. In fact, it is just the opposite. Though not necessarily flattering, their transgressions are among the most common rites of passage. The parent that can't tell stories similar to mine can't tell the truth. Inevitably, the more personal a tale I tell, the more universally it has been experienced. Even from the lectern's distance, I can sense the sympathetic chuckle or chagrined recognition that says the audience knows the story and where it is headed, not because they've heard it before, but because they've lived it. Mostly they are relieved and grateful for confirmation that someone else has lived it too.

When it comes to delivering stories, my children are as reliable as the Sunday *New York Times*. Zach, nearly eighteen, brews mischief the way Starbucks brews coffee. Thankfully, the brew is a mild one, though I suppose that's all relative. If you don't count the accidental possession of a classmate's homemade firebomb, or the juvenile justice hearing for inappropriate intimacy in a public place, or the night the neighbors' roof and trees were toilet papered, or spending the weekend at Alison's when he said he was at Mark's, or totaling the van, there wouldn't actually be that much to tell. They are the kind of stories that are funny years later, once it's clear the survivors have survived, but most were anything but amusing at the time.

My daughter, half past fourteen, heels closer to the straight and narrow. Or maybe it's just that she's learned by watching her brother how to avoid getting caught. Perhaps she plays by the rules only to avoid being speech fodder. But she's just starting high school, so the richest ore has yet to be mined.

After I finish a speech that includes stories of the kids, I usually take questions and then come down from the stage or out from behind the lectern. Typically, a dozen or more folks linger. Some would like a book signed. Others have a question. A handful wait patiently, hesitantly, with a comment they'd prefer the others not hear. They evoke for me the narrator in *The Great Gatsby,* who "realized by some unmistakable sign that an intimate revelation was quivering on the horizon."

The revelation is invariably about their children. If I've spoken for forty minutes, only five were about Zach and Mollie, but that is what they are responding to now. We know almost nothing about each other's professional or personal lives. We are as different as can be in background, income, race, political affiliation, religious belief, temperament. But all parents belong to different chapters of the same fraternity. We want essentially the same things for our kids. Like strangers in a store who reach for the same product at the same time, we stop and smile at each other, knowingly.

What we're reaching for is so basic as to be primal. We want our children to be good and do well. We want them to make the right choices and do the right things, even when no one is looking. We want them to do as we say, not necessarily as we've done, because our doing has been human and invariably flawed. Their purity, on the other hand, is still recent and real enough to be remembered, not relinquished. We want them to attain the higher standards for which we can only strive. We want to make sure they have a compass when we're not there to point the way—that compass being the conscience that will guide them. We want this for reasons that are at once as simple and selfless as a parent's love, and as complex and self-serving as the legacy for which we yearn, the life's work we will not see finished.

And of course the way we parent is critical. As noted author and child psychiatrist Robert Coles has written:

> The conscience does not descend upon us from on high. We learn a convincing sense of right and wrong from parents who are themselves convinced as to what ought to be said and done and under what circumstances, as to what is intolerable, not at all permissible. . . . Without such parents, a conscience is not likely to grow up strong and certain. [A] child can be quite angry at being denied the protection of a strong guiding conscience, at being left morally rudderless.

This common bond among parents is far more significant than the bond I set out to establish for the comparatively trivial sake of holding an audience's attention. This common bond is at the core of our greater evolutionary purpose. It is why seemingly parenthetical stories about my children are central to my words and work. They are not merely to entertain but to underscore what is at stake in the shared human enterprise of searching for meaning, of ensuring that our calling and conscience are one as we strive to bring about the kind of change we'd like to see in the world.

NARROW AND ROCKY STRAITS

WHEN I GET home to Zach and Mollie after a full day's work, I always ask how school was. No answer is more predictable.

"Okay," they say in unison.

"Well, what happened today?"

"Nothing."

"Something must have happened."

"Nope, nothing." They are four years apart in age, and this appears to be one of the rare things on which they agree.

"Did your teachers show up?" If they recognize the question as facetious, they don't show it.

"Yeah."

"Well, what did they talk about?"

"Nothing."

Teenagers are to information as managed care is to health care, parceling out enough to keep you alive but not a drop more. The morsels they share are like sand dollars found on the beach. The sea gives them up when the sea gives them up, impervious to coaxing or encouragement.

Many Americans reduced their travel dramatically after September 11, 2001. I was one of them. But in my case it was not because of the terrorist threat and increased security precautions. It was because that was the month Zach turned sixteen and got his driver's license.

Just a few weeks after he began to drive, Zach asked if he could spend the night with J.P., his best friend in eleventh grade. It seemed as reasonable a request to his mother and me as it must have seemed to J.P.'s parents when J.P. asked if he could spend the night at Mark's house. No one knows exactly what Mark's parents were told, but when this teenage version of three-card monte finally came to an end, Zach, J.P., and Mark were all found under the roof of a friend named Alison. Alison's parents were out of town for the weekend.

The very next night, Zach was more eager than ever to "spend the night at J.P.'s house again." Because I was suspicious, I called J.P.'s mother to make sure she'd be home and to see if I could check in with her first thing in the morning.

When I reached her on Sunday she explained that everything had gone fine. "The only thing that was unusual," she added, "was that around midnight when we went down to tell the boys to settle down and get ready for bed, we discovered this young woman named Alison. We said she had to leave and that Zach could walk her to the car, but that he had to be back inside by twelve-fifteen. Twelve-fifteen came and went. We wanted him back in but we didn't want to embarrass him. I didn't think I should go out and my husband didn't think he should go out, so at twelve-thirty we finally sent J.P." There was a long pause, and then a sigh. "J.P. didn't come back."

Zach's social life began suddenly. It commenced without fanfare, warm-up, or warning. One day he had no social life, and the next day it was full to overflowing. It didn't heat gradually, like a kettle on a stove, but was more like a thrown switch, the kind that bathes a stadium in daylight when just a moment before there was only darkness. Four of Zach's teachers called over the next forty-eight hours to say it seemed Zach was "not focused."

This is what sixteen-year-old boys are wired to do, just as their parents are wired to put up STOP signs, or at least warn of DANGEROUS CURVES. At this age, their stealth and agility are trumped only by the naïveté that precludes realizing their parents can ascertain their every move, not least because they made most of the same moves themselves a mere generation ago. When I confronted Zach about the two episodes involving Alison, he looked at me with incredulity.

"How do you know all of this?"

"I was sixteen once."

"When were you sixteen?" It was an accusation more than a question.

The boys are always surprised that their parents have such a clear picture of what they've been up to, but it is not difficult to piece together the chronology of their adventures. Like bear cubs frolicking through a campground at Yosemite, they are blissfully unaware of the evidence they leave in their wake.

The parents developed their own informal yet sophisticated tracking network, just as pioneers on the frontier, bound by necessity, collaborated to track cattle rustlers. We check with one another by phone before, during, and after our sons' scheduled social activities. Scouting parties just happen to drive by movie theaters and fast-food joints while "on the way to pick up something at the store."

The boys respond with counterespionage strategies designed to maintain their cover. Plans are made over the Internet rather than by phone, to foil eavesdropping attempts. Instant messaging technology is used along with the abbreviated code of Internet vocabulary. Flickering simultaneously across multiple screens, it is unintelligible to anyone beyond the age of eighteen. A conversation disappears into cyberspace with the quick click of a mouse at the first approach of Mom or Dad.

Also, boys constantly change plans at the last minute,

varying routes like experienced fugitives. There have been evenings when they said they were going to a movie but called in from a bat mitzvah party. There have been times they called from the Corner Slice in Bethesda to say they were having a pizza, only to report two days later that the Corner Slice was closed so they had sub sandwiches in Silver Spring instead. Pilots follow the flight plans they've filed with their control tower. Oh, why can't teenage boys?

Many of these skirmishes are just proxy battles in the larger war for independence that is as unavoidable as acne during adolescence. A teenager's job description includes pulling away from parents. A parent's job is not to stop them from pulling away, but to help them distinguish between the right and wrong ways of doing so.

Maintaining sanity as a parent requires drawing from all of the basic Judeo-Christian principles: faith, unconditional love, turning the other cheek, nonviolence in the face of provocation.

Parenthood is like navigating an unwieldy ship through narrow, rocky straits. There is no getting around the straits, only through them. There is no way to speed or slow the passage of craft or child. But a steady hand on the tiller can make the passage smoother. The wrong touch, particularly if impatient or prideful, is apt to make it more harrowing. The best you can do is be present alongside them, and assure them that others have passed this way before.

SNOW JOB

IN MID-DECEMBER of 2002, after Washington's first snow, I returned from several days of business travel to the arduous task of shoveling snow from my sidewalk and driveway, as well as those of my elderly neighbor. An hour into it, straining from the exertion, I thought I'd take a break to see what had accumulated in the mailbox while I was gone. I should have known better.

Amid the usual bills and flyers was a thick envelope from the Washington Waldorf School, where my son, Zach, is a senior. The school frequently mails home event calendars and various notices. This envelope had a rectangular cellophane window, through which showed my address. The only other words that could be seen were: "Dear Mr. Shore, On Friday, November 22, Zach made the unfortunate choice to. . . ." The rest of the sentence ran behind the envelope.

Shoveling snow suddenly seemed less of a strain. I stood in the middle of my street, blanketed white, silent and still, and debated whether to open the letter. I made a mental list of Zach's most recent unfortunate choices. At least the subset I was aware of. I cross-checked it against those within a five-mile radius of his school. Hmmm . . . yep, I could guess.

While out of town on business, I let Zach use my car. It is a 1994 Jeep Cherokee with 150,000 miles on it, and new brakes, tires, and transmission in anticipation of my son behind the wheel. In Maslow's hierarchy of needs, those of teenage boys narrow to one: a car.

All I asked of Zach was that he be careful, make curfew, and not ride with more than one friend in the Jeep at a time. His failure to protest any of these restrictions should have triggered warning bells.

It was the restrictions I neglected to impose that were the problem. For school the next day, Zach needed the car for less than an hour. At least, that was how long it sat idle from the time he drove it to school until the moment after first period when he drove it away to the nearest shopping mall. Even worse, he soon returned to the scene of the crime, triggering his suspension for the day, calls to his parents from the principal, and the wounded look of the unjustly accused on Zach's otherwise untroubled face.

So I had a good idea what the letter was about. With the walk finally shoveled clean, parental responsibility got the better of me. I wedged the orange blade of my shovel into a drift so that it stood upright in the snow, went inside, pulled off my boots, and turned my attention to the envelope and the gory details of its indictment.

The Waldorf School's standard practice is to send preprinted disciplinary forms home with check marks indicating tardiness or other breaches of school rules. There is a perfunctory nature to them, as if someone with just enough legal education to be dangerous was creating a paper trail in case the school administrators invoked more drastic measures. No one takes them too seriously. This letter, however, was more formal, addressing me as Mr. Shore, and went into considerable detail. Its author, high school chair Linda Sawers, clearly labored under the same dilemma that so often perplexed Zach's mother and me: a mountain of circumstantial evidence, but no smoking gun.

According to the letter, Zach not only left school but also took a classmate with him, returned "through the exit driveway," and "at a rate of speed that caught the attention of a teacher." The even-handed Ms. Sawers also summarized Zach's defense: "To Zach's credit, he was cooperative and apologetic about his deeds. He claimed he did not know he had broken the rules, and he thought others had been given permission to leave. We found that Zach had permission to leave class to get a drink of water. He was expected to do just that, stay in the building and return to class. So, the decisions that Zach made remain puzzling."

"Puzzling." I can picture Zach suppressing a smile. "Puzzling" he can live with. "Puzzling" is the loophole he's driven trucks through all of his life. And now a Jeep. There is nothing illegal about "puzzling." "Puzzling" triggers no onerous sanctions. If the worst they have on him is "puzzling," well then, next case.

Later that day I spoke to Zach about the letter, and the entire incident. Careful not to overreact in a way that would reinforce suspicion, he just chuckled, as if at the pettiness of the school administrators in contrast to his own worldly maturity. But he also casually but firmly insisted it had all been a big misunderstanding. No one had said he couldn't run to the mall after first period. No, I'm sure no one thought to. Also, a rumor had been circulating that there was some kind of early dismissal in the works.

Neither of us doubted he would once again beat the rap. His string of acquittals at the expense of both principals and parents was uncanny. It made me recall watching Perry Mason when I was very young and wondering how his counterpart, state's attorney Hamilton Berger, could bear always losing, night after night, always starting out so self-assured and then seeing defeat snatched from the jaws of victory, as if it had been preordained.

Then it dawned on me just how much Zach and Perry Mason had in common. As disappointed as I was with the decisions Zach made, I found consolation in realizing that he had learned something far more valuable than whatever was being taught in second period at Waldorf. Indeed, Zach was the living embodiment of the philosophy at the core of the American system, a fundamental freedom that men had fought and died to secure. He had an intuitive understanding of, and deep abiding faith in, that bedrock of Anglo-American jurisprudence: innocent until proven guilty beyond a reasonable doubt.

For all of the ambiguities that have surfaced in Zach's explanations over the years, the one thing he understands unambiguously is burden of proof. He need not prove his innocence. Indeed he rarely even bothers going through the motions of trying to do so. The burden is rather on others to prove his guilt. Not accuse or imply, or even persuade, but prove beyond a reasonable doubt. It is this standard that has been the salvation of persecuted minorities, unpopular activists, innocent victims, and teenagers like Zach.

For the most part, he avoids the potential pitfalls inherent in any alibi—contradictions, loopholes, lack of sufficient verification—by not risking the construction of one.

Boys Zach's age are masters of obfuscation and deception. If Saddam Hussein were a teenager, we'd have had no chance of ever pinning weapons of mass destruction on him. There would be at least a plausibility that they belonged to someone else, that the dictator next door had asked him to keep them for him, that he really didn't know how they got there.

Kids know the difference between telling the truth and telling a lie, between right and wrong. They have the ability to make those distinctions from a very young age. What they don't have is the ability to foresee the consequences when they choose the path they know is wrong, to foresee that dishonesty will eventually catch up with them. That's the moral equivalent of being able to see around corners. And while none of us can do that, as we get older, experience teaches that there will be something around the corner to deal with.

That's why a child's best compass is a conscience, and a

parent's most important job is to teach the child to trust that true north is where the quivering needle says it is. How many times have you been driving somewhere and lost confidence in the accuracy of the directions, so instead charted your own course? How many times have you regretted doing so? Children are born with a conscience, just not with the wisdom and experience to abide it. That's where parenting comes in.

Every stage of parenting has its challenges. Some are made bearable only by the fact that they are just that: phases, with a beginning, middle, and end. Therefore each arrives with a promise in tow—like a train with engines at both ends—that it will also, in due time, go.

Parents, of course, expect to be the conductors of the train. But by the time kids pass their mid-teens, the trains start to leave the station when they want, for where they want. If we're lucky, some of what we've tried to impart will stay hitched on like a caboose, something they can look back at, something they know will follow them wherever they go.

REACHING HIGHER

I HELD MY breath as I stood thirty feet below Mollie, watching her hang from a ledge by her fingertips. From the shoulders down she twisted and turned, wrenching her hips, her feet desperately seeking something solid upon which to light. I was silent, as were those watching with me below.

On Saturday mornings I drive Mollie and her friend Jenna to Sportrock in suburban Maryland. Some parents complain about constantly chauffeuring their children about, but I look for such opportunities. Children are never more relaxed or chatty than in the backseat of a car. Toss in a friend or two and you hear things you would otherwise never hear.

Mollie and Jenna are eleven and have been friends since day care. They share play dates, a Sunday school teacher, drama practice, and an obsession with boy bands. During our ride, they discussed MTV's rumor that 'N Sync star Justin Timberlake had assaulted a female fan. Mollie has been to two 'N Sync concerts, arriving and leaving with her parents but virtually disappearing while there, replaced by a shrieking, bobbing, swaying pre-teen who knows the words to every song. Certain their idol was unjustly accused, the girls offered defenses as they speculated about how his appreciation of their loyalty would manifest itself, if only he knew.

"We didn't have those problems when I was in a band," I said casually. Mollie ignored the comment, but in the rearview mirror I saw Jenna's head snap in my direction. This knack for conversation stoppers is one I came by honestly. When I was Mollie's age my father regularly made passing references to playing with the Brooklyn Dodgers. We asked questions of him for hours, not for the answers, which we didn't believe, but for the fun of testing his inventiveness and to see if we could stump him.

In the front seat next to me, Mollie tilted her head against the window in resignation. She rolled her eyes. She knew what would happen next and knew she couldn't prevent it. Her friend Jenna was the only accomplice I needed.

"Were you really in a band, Mr. Shore?"

"Mr. *what*?" I corrected her.

"Mr. Wallet," she said brightly, responding to my coaching.

"That's better."

Parents assume overlapping roles in their children's lives, transitioning from one to another as the need arises, the way cabinet officials serving a president move from Treasury to the State Department when needed. Dads range across playmate, baby-sitter, coach, confidant, repairman, and mentor. My current role is central banker. I am the Alan Greenspan of Mollie's circumscribed but expensive universe, regulating her money supply with a calm yet firm hand, liberal enough not to create panic, conservative enough to ensure at least the veneer of fiscal responsibility. I simplified this for Jenna, explaining that Mollie thinks of her dad only as a wallet, and for consistency's sake I'd prefer to be addressed that way.

"Were you really in a band, Mr. Wallet?" Jenna grinned broadly, as if the word itself tickled.

"Oh, of course."

"What did you play?"

I hesitated for a moment, but Mollie had heard all this before.

"He played the teakettle," she said, rolling her eyes again. As with the bedtime stories I used to make up, she remembers the details better than I do. She will catch and correct the slightest deviation. It appears I have two accomplices.

"The teakettle?" Jenna asked, confused.

"Yes, the teakettle," I repeated, as matter-of-factly as possible, confident I knew where to go from there. There was only a moment's uncertainty left before she played along with gusto.

"How did you play the teakettle, Mr. Wallet?" Jenna asked.

I whistled, high-pitched and off key. "Like that." I demonstrated with one hand on my hip and the other imitating a spout. "I can assure you it's harder than it looks."

I returned both hands to the steering wheel and glanced at Mollie out of the corner of my eye. She couldn't decide whether she was embarrassed or amused. It would depend largely on Jenna's reaction.

"And you never had problems with your fans?" Jenna asked, easing into the role of straight man and circling back to where we started.

"No, but they were much older."

"How old?"

"Mostly in their seventies and eighties. Women whose husbands were dead, but who still wanted to go to rock concerts. They didn't cause much trouble. We made them check their walkers at the door."

At Jenna's request I performed a few tunes, ad-libbing with

my whistle, and then described our typical concert and some of our more outrageous encores. They giggled for the rest of the ride.

It was only a temporary respite in what had become for Mollie a near obsession with boy bands.

At eleven, Mollie is halfway to adulthood. She is woman, pre-teen, and little girl all in one package, like a set of Russian dolls in which one incarnation hides within another. In the morning she still snuggles like a newborn cub in her mother's lap until awake. Not an hour later she walks out the front door, head held high like a runway model who never looks back. Old enough for a bra but young enough to wear it beneath Curious George jerseys. She is tall for her age, with brown hair, long and thick, that she brushes with a concentration that Grandmasters reserve for the chess board.

Her sweetness is leavened with the intensity of a Wall Street trader. She knows no gradations between her wants. She bargains for a horse and a guinea pig with matching, relentless vigor. A kid's meal at McDonald's and a new CD player are of equal value when they are what she wants in the moment. Likewise, the consequences of whatever she's denied are equal as well. Each and every deprivation will "ruin my life forever" and prove "I have the strictest parents in the whole world."

Eleven is the age when self-esteem is held hostage to the opinions of friends, classmates, and even strangers about hair, hands, height, weight, skin, and clothes. Because her sense of self is fragile, Mollie logically operates on the assumption that the affections of others are as volatile and as subject to influence as hers. She has the biggest heart in the family, but has always had trouble finding the line between generosity and buying affection. When choosing a present for the bat mitzvah of her friend Amanda, Mollie ordered an 'N Sync poster with the "certified" signatures of the entire band. She did not ask in advance what it would cost, and after it arrived was not fazed by the $240 price tag. I could not let her go through with it.

"But, Dad, I told all of my friends I was getting this for Amanda. It will ruin everything if I don't."

"Two hundred and forty dollars is a lot of money, Molls."

"I can pay for it myself," she offers, affirming that the new economy includes children too.

"That's not the point, honey."

"Then what *is* the point?" She punctuates this by slapping her leg.

"The point is to learn something about the value of things," I say, but I know I'm not articulating this well.

"But it's not for me, Dad. I'm doing it for someone else."

This is relevant but not mitigating, although I am unsuccessful in drawing the distinction.

"It's just not right for you to spend that much of your money that way."

"Aaugh!" she screams in despair. "But that's the whole point: It's my money!"

It's a conversation we've had before, about material gifts, their value, and our values. For example, her older brother's approval is highly sought, and if left to her own devices she would shower him with gifts. We once endured a daylong standoff over her insistence on buying him an expensive marble chess set. Zach does not play chess. She was undeterred.

Where does she get this? Since I silently take credit for her many positive attributes, I can't be exempt from owning the shortcomings. I think of the times I've tried to compensate for my extensive travel by bringing her a special gift, about my inability to say no whenever there is anything she wants to buy. About why her friends call me "Mr. Wallet." She may come by it honestly.

As I write about Mollie and her brother, Zach, again and again, I begin to understand why some painters return time after time to the same bowl of fruit, or landscape, or model. Andrew Wyeth painted his neighbor Helga asleep at least a dozen times. Monet painted haystacks and cathedrals in different lights and different seasons. Only by looking from so many angles and coming back again and again can you begin to understand, let alone capture, their true nature. In a letter to his son, the painter Camille Pissarro wrote: "It is only by drawing often, drawing everything, drawing incessantly, that one fine day you discover to your surprise, that you have rendered something in its true character."

The same is true for writing, and if I write about the kids again and again it is not just to render their true character but to know it. They reveal different facets in different seasons and light. But some of their revelations are so subtle and fleeting, like childhood itself, as to be evanescent. Catch and keep them like leaves in wax paper pressed between pages of a book, or they crumble and dissolve away. Writing is the literary equivalent of staring. It allows one to look longer. I once felt reluctance bordering on guilt to use my time with the children to enhance my writing, but I know now that I use my writing to enhance my time with and knowledge of the children.

Mollie and Jenna do their rock climbing indoors at an unmarked warehouse in Rockville, Maryland, where a business called Sportrock flourishes. Wedged tightly into a row of nondescript buildings in a back alley, it looks like a bankruptcy court's idea of how to salvage condemned property. The business consists of about a dozen rocky-looking walls, each forty feet high, with small variously colored knobs, ledges, crevices, and handholds built into them.

When you arrive at Sportrock, they fit you with a safety harness that tethers you to a rope looped around a bar on the ceiling. In theory it prevents serious falls. For the next two hours you climb, grasp, hang, stretch, and otherwise struggle mightily to get to the top of the walls. What makes this a business is that you actually pay for this privilege of hanging by your fingertips at great heights.

The first wall is for a warm-up and is the easiest climb of

the day. Jenna went first and she was at the top in seconds. Mollie followed. This was the order they maintained throughout the afternoon, but soon the going got tougher.

On the next wall, Jenna thought strategically about where to put hands and feet. She had the strength to follow through. She scaled rapidly and with a confidence that compensated for her diminutive size. When Mollie's turn came it was a slower process. She was unsure and cautious. But also determined. She might not go higher, but she would never come down on her own. It wouldn't faze her to bring all of Sportrock to a halt for the rest of the day if that's how long it took her to finish. At times she was suspended in a single spot for five to ten minutes as she scoured the wall for options.

As the day went on, the climbs got tougher and tougher, especially for Mollie. The more advanced walls were not just steep but concave. Jenna, to her credit, encouraged her generously from the ground. "You got it, Mollie, come on, you can do it, reach, Mollie, reach." Jenna and I and an instructor all stood there, heads tilted, rocking back on our heels, willing Mollie to get to the top.

When I first walked into this renovated warehouse, it seemed like something other than sport, silly and artificially contrived. But as I watched the young men and women whose agility and fitness I envy, I began to appreciate the athleticism involved. It is a developmental smorgasbord that any parent would wish for a child: skill, judgment, coordination, strength, and ultimately confidence. Best of all, it's fun.

But something less obvious was happening here too. As Mollie pulled herself from one handhold to the next, she pulled that much further away from boy bands, peer pressure, and anyone else's sense of who she is and what she's capable of.

Though she couldn't see or understand it at the time, if Mollie continues to learn her way around and over walls like these, she'll find that her joys and triumphs can't be given or bought, but instead lie within her as they always have and always will.

Parents seek to instill values and conscience in their children. There is no set formula. Of all we wish our kids to learn and be, this challenge comes without handbook, class, or methodology. It takes more than sermons, lectures, punishments, and even role models. But a foundation can be laid of independence, strength, and sure-footedness. Such a foundation serves many ends. Sometimes abiding one's conscience will feel as alone as Mollie feels hanging on to that wall. The sooner she realizes she has the strength to survive and surmount that, the better.

Our time at Sportrock was almost up. As Mollie got nearer and nearer the top, she slowed even more, if that's possible, inching up the wall barely faster than a vine might grow. But I was in no hurry. Because each step was also taking her one step farther from me, and the work of a parent is never finished.

III

Conscience Sets the Agenda

A conscience that does not speak up when injustices are being committed is betraying itself. A mute conscience is a false conscience.

—ELIE WIESEL

TIPPING POINT FOR THE WORLD

IT'S AN HOUR past noon, and high tide at Goose Rocks Beach. The waves slap gently but insistently at the shore. Softly enough not to disturb the tranquillity, but loudly enough to ensure their presence won't go unnoticed. From a second-story deck on Kings Highway, the view is all greens and blues.

Nothing defines *steady* more convincingly than these waves. Nothing is more immune to fashion, or culture's fickle shifts, or man's hubris. Stay away a season or stay away a century, you know what you'll find when you come back. The tides are a promise that makes up for our own unsureness, a sympathetic friend that won't mock us when we come unmoored or lose our rhythms, for the ocean knows swells and storms as well. It models reassurance that our rhythm will return, that harmony is as predictable and as natural as the absence of harmony.

It was here in January 2000 that I sat and read of Vermont senator James Jeffords's announcement that he was leaving the Republican party. The move shifted control of the previously evenly divided Senate from the Republicans to the Democrats. It was the banner headline of almost every newspaper in the country, because of the massive change it set in motion and because of the drama of public anguish it stirred in the sixty-seven-year-old politician.

In the second sentence of his statement, Jeffords referred to the role of conscience in his decision. He affirmed his love for Vermont and placed the state in context as one of "independence and social conscience." It's no coincidence that he married these words. David Shribman, writing in *The Boston Globe,* said Jeffords "has given new life to one of the sturdiest caricatures of craggy, up-country New England, the region's colorful if stubborn strain of independence. . . . By breaking the most enduring rule of Washington—above all, don't double-cross your party—he has changed all the rules of American politics."

How fascinating that an act experienced as a double-cross by almost half of Jeffords's colleagues was witnessed as an act of conscience by the other half.

In a widely quoted passage from his statement, Jeffords

explained: "It has become a struggle for our leaders to deal with me and for me to deal with them." This makes his decision sound like an act more of mutual convenience than of moral conscience.

Whether Jeffords gained personally or professionally by his action is subject to conflicting interpretations. He surely lost some old friends and may never be completely trusted by his new ones. On the other hand, he may have gained some choice committee assignments and the perks and privileges that go with them. If his decision served his self-interest, was it still an act of conscience? Maybe the real test is not one of selflessness or selfishness, not one of making the right choice or the wrong, but rather choosing to listen to one's own counsel rather than be swayed by other voices, loud and powerful as those that descended on Jeffords, up to and including that of the President of the United States.

Acts of conscience are often close calls between viable arguments on both sides and even competing voices deep within. We rarely have the luxury of knowing in advance which course will prove to be right in the long term. The only luxury of which we can be assured is that of looking back and knowing that we were at least true to ourselves.

Soon the stories about Jeffords began to recede from the news in favor of the larger analysis of what his action meant for the Senate as an institution. I know that institution, having worked there, and virtually lived there, for thirteen years. Acts of conscience are admired, like Vermeer paintings, not only for their beauty but because they are so rare, a politician's version of a collector's item.

In contemporary times, the senator most associated with following his conscience was Philip Hart of Michigan. He died shortly before I began working on Capitol Hill. But I'd heard my employer, Senator Gary Hart (no relation), invoke his name often, and once in a pointed way.

As one of Senator Hart's half-dozen legislative assistants, it was my job to track legislation in certain issue areas and recommend how he vote on the numerous bills and amendments that came to the Senate floor for roll call votes.

Sometimes it was clear for days in advance what the Senate would be working on, but often senators would draft amendments on the spot, allowing little preparation before a vote that could be part of the senator's permanent record. An "aye" or "nay" follows you for the rest of your career in elective politics, so it's important to understand what you're voting on and to get it right.

Senator Hart wanted a written memo in advance of every roll call vote. It was to include a description of the issue, an analysis of the consequences, the impact on Colorado, and a consolidated staff recommendation on how he ought to vote. I took these memos very seriously, no doubt a reflection of taking myself very seriously, and assumed that the fate of the free world could ride on the outcome, as well as the equally weighty fate of Hart's next re-election bid. He of course had many other sources to draw on that I was all but oblivious to, including his conversations with other senators, his own voting record on many of the same issues in the years before I joined his staff, and his wide-ranging reading.

The tougher votes were those that could not be prepared for in advance. Advising on these required a careful and constant monitoring of the debates and proceedings on the Senate floor. The Senate was not televised in those days, so instead we listened through the "squawk box," a closed-circuit audio transmission that was broadcast throughout the entire Senate complex like Muzak.

In a very short time one came to recognize all one hundred senators by their voices. The Senate still had a few august figures in those days, or perhaps the familiarity of television had not yet bred contempt. But there were several senators of both parties whose voices made you stop what you were doing and gather around the box to listen carefully because what you were about to hear would have logic and weight and might possibly be historic. Senators like Abe Ribicoff of Connecticut, Jacob Javits of New York, Hart of Michigan, William Fulbright of Arkansas, and Henry "Scoop" Jackson of Washington.

None of them was perfect. All were political creatures not oblivious to their own political survival. But each had a farsightedness his colleagues lacked—an ability to see and articulate and put first the larger national interest.

Sometimes even careful listening was insufficient. The full text of an amendment is not always read aloud. Its meaning might depend upon background documents, or upon which clause of a bill it is amending. The only way to understand it fully might be to run over to the Senate gallery or the floor itself.

Then, when the one long buzz was sounded signifying a roll call vote, I would race to the elevators that opened nearest the Senate chamber. Not knowing where Hart would be coming from and not sure of any other way to reach him, I'd stand there poised to spit out in rapid fire what the issues were and which way he should cast his vote, careful to include political qualifiers like "Kennedy and Rockefeller are voting against it" or "The NAACP is for it."

Once, knowing that the majority of Coloradans were opposed to an expensive urban transportation bill that was nevertheless good public policy and would pass by a wide margin whether or not Hart voted for it, I committed what he considered a cardinal sin by advising: "You can vote against this because it is going to pass anyway."

Hart gave me a stern look, then softened, perhaps recognizing that I was only doing my job as it had long been defined, and said, "Philip Hart always said you should cast every vote as if it were the deciding vote, as if it would tip the entire roll call one way or the other. That's how I want to cast mine."

There is a teaching in Judaism that the world is perfectly balanced between good and evil and that you should live your life as if each action can and will have the consequence of tipping it irretrievably in one direction or the other. Neither Philip Hart nor Gary Hart was Jewish, and it's unlikely they'd had direct exposure to this tenet of Talmudic teaching, but it was the philosophy they applied to their Senate duties.

Columnist Colman McCarthy labeled Philip Hart the most trusted man of American politics: "How many owed something to Hart when he died Sunday can't be known, but it can be said that because of the moral substance of his positions and the depth of his character, it was not an accident that he was the most trusted man of American politics. He fronted for no one. His alliances were to timeless ideals, not upstart lobbies. As though he were the wildest of gamblers, he bet that the common vanities of hack politics—images, smiles, calls for brighter days—counted for little. Instead, he wagered that conscience and persistence could matter."

This Judaic creed, however, is not just about the altruism of saving the world. It also directly affects the quality of one's own life, because one continues to live in the world that is either saved or doomed. And so not only is the fate of the world in the hands of the doer, but so is the doer's fate.

THE LIGHT OF HUMAN CONSCIENCE

WHEN I WORKED on a Senate staff on Capitol Hill, my job was to respond rapidly to breaking news. It was the role I created for myself. I scoured the newspapers in search of social ills that needed a remedy or innovative ideas that needed a mouthpiece. And I found them. Whether it was a cut in food stamps that needed to be reversed or a new solar energy technology that could be encouraged through federal tax credits, there were many mornings that I'd drafted legislation responding to something I'd read in the papers even before Senator Hart got to his desk. I acted on the principle that if I had a certain idea, then some other eager beaver in the sprawling complex of House and Senate office buildings probably had it too. So speed was essential, first in clarifying the idea, and then in staking a claim that would enable it to be associated unmistakably with the senator for whom I worked.

The system was deceptively simple. Behind the formalities of parliamentary procedure and "If the gentleman would yield . . . ," the Congress operated on the basis of unwritten and informal customs that would have shocked the unsuspecting outsider. An amendment to the body of public law bound in red leather volumes could be written on the back of an envelope—even on a cocktail napkin—introduced that way, and voted upon.

My goal was to sharpen my skills so that I acted reflexively, without even thinking. Reacting quickly and clearly in ways that had political appeal was a rare skill. After a few years of experience, I felt I was at the top of my game. But that was only a young man's illusion. Because an even rarer skill is not in reacting but in defining what others react to. It means developing a point of view and having the confidence, stubbornness, and courage to anchor to it. There are two kinds of leadership: derivative and original. The most powerful leadership is that which defines the agenda.

Like so many young people who arrive in Washington, D.C., I started out filled with idealism, interning on Capitol Hill, doing research and other inconsequential chores that the backdrop of the Capitol made seem incredibly consequential. I was convinced that the enactment of a bill or amendment into law was the most powerful way to create change. And while I'm still an idealist and still believe in the efficacy of public policy, I see now that the legislation is the end point, that I had started at the finish line rather than the place where the course of the race could be most influenced. Now, step by step, I've backed all the way up to the beginning. The great change makers—Gandhi, King, Mandela—weren't legislators at all. They were the people who created the demand for change. They were the architects. The lawmakers were their general contractors, laboring to ensure that the construction was faithful to their vision.

Now at middle age and in the second half of my career at Share Our Strength, I marvel at where twenty years have gone and know more certainly than I did in my youth that not only won't the job be finished in my lifetime, but it cannot be accomplished alone. The task at hand is not just to do the work, but to create both the motivation and the vehicles for as many others to get involved as possible.

Real social change is incredibly difficult to achieve. Obstacles range from complacency and inertia to powerful vested interests always aligned on behalf of the status quo. Change agents, almost by definition, never get to play on the team with the most resources. While we are fond of arguing that we can make a little go a long way, the truth is that a little just goes a little way. The only thing that goes a long way is a lot. A career spent in pursuit of social change becomes a lifelong search for greater leverage, for determining where one's own efforts can have the greatest impact.

I believed at first that that place was in government service, that drafting and passing legislation in Washington was the best way to bring about change. From the time I could read, my father would bring home copies of the *Congressional Record* and I would pore over the triple columns of small print that reflected the glory of great debate on the topics of the day ranging from the war in Vietnam to civil rights.

My deepest reason for exploring conscience is that it is ultimately the seed from which all change grows, the foundation for activism and reform. Until the conscience of an individual or society is moved, the requisite motivation and energy for making any change is lacking.

This principle comes across nowhere more clearly than in the recent biography of Dr. Martin Luther King, Jr., by Marshall Frady. The great victories of the civil rights era were impossible until King's strategy of "surfacing tensions" made it impossible for individuals to hide from their own consciences. "In his 'letter from a Birmingham jail,'" writes Frady, "Dr. King describes his hopes for a strike and boycott: 'Injustice must be exposed, with all the tensions its exposure creates, to the light of human conscience and the air of national opinion before it can be cured.'"

The very intentional strategy behind enactment of the Public Accommodations Act, which desegregated the South, and the Voting Rights Act, which forever shifted the balance of political power, was to demonstrate "the power of right . . . to rouse the larger community to shame and redress." Frady traces King's own journey, explaining that

> becoming further captivated with Thoreau's proposition that "one honest man" could morally regenerate an entire society, King then discovered Gandhi, and the way he transformed Thoreau's principle of individual nonviolent resistance into a seismic popular movement to expunge British power from India, through the enormous "soul force" of a patiently suffering mass resistance, impossibly inconveniencing not only the administrative agencies but the conscience of its rulers.

HINGES OF HOPE

BUMPER STICKERS USUALLY make you smile. Some can make you cry. That's what I discovered after driving hundreds of miles through the poorest parts of the Mississippi Delta and the Rio Grande Valley to witness firsthand how some of our fellow Americans live.

. . .

It wasn't the poverty in the dying towns of the Delta that got me, nor the crowded housing conditions for the children of migrant workers from the colonias, who are even sweeter than the fruit their fathers pick. I was prepared for both. What I wasn't prepared for was a single green bumper sticker. It was just like the kind I've seen so many times before. But it was where I saw it that made all the difference.

If America's economy boomed in the last decade, nobody told them in the boarded-up towns which dot the Mississippi Delta, where they joke that even the prisoners won't stay. A thirty-million-dollar prison built by a private company and expected to generate jobs closed shortly after it opened when Wisconsin reneged on its decision to export prisoners there and brought them all back.

I first visited the Delta six years ago because it was where Dr. Martin Luther King, Jr., began the Poor People's Campaign. Little has changed since, except for the new casinos built in Tunica County. But for most who live in the Delta, if it weren't for bad luck they wouldn't have any luck at all. Women still collect rainwater in cisterns, but because of the lack of sanitation, become desperately ill from leeches. A high school senior struggling to get students to after-school and summer school programs drives a "might van"—"it might get us there and it might not."

But poor doesn't mean ordinary. The challenging conditions attract amazing people who have committed their lives to ameliorating them. These are places I think of as "hinges of hope," encompassing both despair and promise. The door could swing either way. If we can impact its direction, hope could flow freely instead of being locked out.

Our delegation included executives from American Express and Tyson Foods, and New York restaurateur Danny Meyer and Chicago restaurateur Susan Goss, and Scott Wilkerson (owner of many Lincoln-Mercury dealerships), among other successful entrepreneurs. At the new community center, which is the pride of Tutwiler, we found 1968 Olympic gold medalist Mildrette Graves sharing her strength by teaching physical education to kids in a beautiful gymnasium. Next door is Sister Anne Brooks, one of three doctors in Tallahatchie County, at the clinic she built. An amazing woman who became a doctor at age forty after spending eighteen years in a wheelchair for arthritis, Sister Brooks has been in Tutwiler for twenty years, waging a lonely battle against diabetes, hypertension, teen pregnancy, and similar local afflictions that are accepted as inevitable but are in fact preventable.

The Rio Grande Valley is quite a contrast to the Mississippi Delta. Dry, brown, and dusty where the Delta is fertile and green, its economy is booming, driven by a population explosion and a porous border with Mexico. The town of McAllen, which served as our base, is home to the top two

Wal-Mart stores in the country. Only the migrant workers, who pick the food we enjoy, are left behind.

We traveled with David Arizmendi, then executive director of Proyecto Azteca, which provides affordable housing by training teams of families to assemble prefabricated three-bedroom homes to replace their migrant shacks. They produce almost eighty homes a year. Marveling at the spirit of the people, he asks: "If you are a migrant worker making $7,000 a year, where do you get off thinking you can buy a home?" But, he explains, the people are filled with "the idea that the future is going to be better. That is their mind-set. And so they buy a little land. And in a year they may have been able to buy three boards. And then next year another three. But eventually they have a home."

A sense of optimism pervades the Valley, and a culture of achievement. A charter school called the IDEA Academy, started by a Teach for America alum, has the strictest rules but the highest test scores in the Valley. A schoolteacher tells us he is revered among the migrant families in a way teachers in the rest of the United States typically are not.

The migrant workers cluster into unincorporated neighborhoods called *colonias*. They are part of no city and have no city services. Not water or paved roads, not streetlights or street numbers. No post office either. A siren blasts when the mail truck comes. Here the West is still wild. An abandoned bus might be home as surely as a few boards cobbled together. The yards and streets are littered with stripped and abandoned cars. Dogs are chained everywhere, the colonia's security system.

Our visit to one colonia began at a new community center. We were greeted by Mrs. Ochoa, a neatly dressed young mother who welcomed us through a translator. Children sat quietly drawing at a corner table while other mothers offered cookies and cola and described what the community center had meant to them. When we left, the sun was high and the full heat of the Valley was upon us.

David Arizmendi drove us through the colonias, and though it was our third such sojourn, it was still riveting, like the train wreck you can't look away from. We pulled up at one particularly small house and David said we'd be going inside.

Really? I wondered.

"Yes, no problem. It is Mrs. Ochoa's," he explained, as if reading my mind.

"Who?"

"The woman who welcomed you at the center. She is already here to greet you."

I thought there must be some mistake. That woman was so nicely dressed, and so well-spoken, so happy. How could she live here? The house consisted of two small, dark bedrooms, each about the size of a walk-in closet. One room had two mattresses on the floor and a TV on a dresser. Five small children stared at it from a corner of one of the mattresses. The other room had four mattresses on bunk beds, and a dresser on which stood an array of cosmetics and one large trophy.

The heat was stifling. The house was so small we had to take turns going in, like a stateroom in a Marx Brothers movie, only without the laugh track. The oldest son, maybe twelve, came in and held the trophy proudly. I asked if it was for basketball, but he pointed to the plaque: "Top Ten Students." His younger sister's smile flashed two silver teeth, an early sign of poor nutrition.

I walked to our van and the yard dust swirled. I turned to look at the house again. It was just a shack, really. Something green affixed to the wooden front door, perfectly centered, caught my eye. I stepped toward it. It was a bumper sticker that read "Proud Parent of a Farias Elementary School Honor Student."

It stopped me in my tracks. It was almost identical to those I see in Bethesda, Maryland, and Alexandria, Virginia, on SUVs kept in garages more than twice the size of Mrs. Ochoa's home. The bumper sticker told me more about her than she'd been able to. A woman who I thought had nothing, instead had what was most important—a pride, both gentle and fierce, in her truest measure as an American: the better life she was creating for her children. But that green bumper sticker was even more than that. It was a banner of hope in a generation. As that door swung back and forth on its rusty hinges, hope swung with it.

There are two kinds of poverty in America. There are those who don't have. And there are those who don't know. I've seen one. I've been the other. At least until my trip to the Mississippi Delta and the Rio Grande Valley.

Nothing is more important to our ability to fight hunger and poverty and social injustice with the passion the task requires than the ongoing ability to feel something. After eighteen years of this work, I'm almost numb to statistics, grant proposals, and case studies. I don't always even trust my eyes and ears. But my heart has yet to fail me, though at times it may ache.

Our first order of business is not challenging others to do more, but challenging ourselves to feel more, to resist the comforts of office, home, and backyard barbecue, and to force ourselves to all but trespass among those whose dialect is as different from ours as their skin color, whose opportunities may seem as constricted as their homes but whose children are every bit as precious.

Even long after I'm back home, I know that a thousand miles away a nun presses a stethoscope against the chest of a man in a county short of doctors, and a carpenter presses a nail into the prefabricated home that will free a family from the squalor of the colonias, and even in those colonias where thousands are still left behind, some mother is proudly pressing a bumper sticker against a door whose hinges open just wide enough to let in hope.

Washington Post columnist David Broder wrote an Independence Day column about the late John Gardner, the author, teacher, cabinet secretary, and founder of Common Cause, whom he quoted at length, including:

> I keep running into highly capable potential leaders all over this country who literally never give a thought to the well-being of their community. And I keep wondering who gave them permission to stand aside! I'm asking you to issue a wake-up call to those people—a bugle call right in their ear. And I want you to tell them that this nation could die of comfortable indifference to the problems that only citizens can solve. Tell them that.

I can't think of a better way to describe the purpose behind the trip described above. The people in Marks, Mississippi, know what Gardner means by "comfortable indifference." We had a breakfast meeting with several dozen local leaders. I said we'd come to Marks because we believed that the hardest challenges produce the most amazing people to meet them, and that we not only wanted to learn from those people, but also felt that there is value in trying to break out of our comfort zones, get out of our own backyards, and find ways to meet people who talk differently, look different, and have very different lives, but who share this country as fellow human beings. If we're not capable of anything else, we can all at least try to do that. Suddenly, heads began to nod.

Sixty minutes from Memphis but half a century from the American mainstream, the Mississippi Delta produces an overwhelming sensation of isolation. Our hosts told us that their towns of three thousand see visitors from outside Mississippi maybe twice a year. What is true everywhere is magnified there. Nothing changes until someone cares, and no one cares until someone sees. There are no simple solutions to the problems these communities face. But there are simple first steps toward citizen engagement: seeing, knowing, feeling.

My work has always been aimed at attracting new people to the cause. Instead of preaching to the choir, I've tried to recruit for it. That happens only when individual consciences embrace a dual realization: first that there is a need, and second, that they themselves can actually play some meaningful role in meeting that need. If conscience is the coin of the realm, those are its two sides. Throughout history it has been the common currency for down payments on organizations ranging from the Red Cross to the United Farm Workers, from Share Our Strength to City Year. The rest is small change.

For a long time I reflexively believed that legislation, programs, new agencies, and more dollars were the appropriate response to social problems. But they are more like the tools to implement the response.

So much energy goes into legislating what people can and cannot do, like efforts far downstream to channel waters that have already taken on a course and speed of their own. Far too little is spent at the headwaters, on creating experiences that will determine what people want to do and how they want to conduct themselves. The kind of leadership that seeks to inspire rather than control has at its foundation a faith in the conscience of people, that the more they know the more likely they are to do the right thing.

Gardner wrote: "Most Americans welcome the voice that lifts them out of themselves. They want to be better people. They want to help make this a better country. When the American spirit awakens, it transforms the world. But it does not awaken without a challenge."

A GOOD CONSCIENCE HIS ONLY SURE REWARD

ON A RAINY Tuesday morning in South Bend, Indiana, just a few days past Thanksgiving, a small boy is walking slowly, aimlessly down the street. The expression on his face is casual, almost blank, his steps tentative, and his eyes mask apprehension no child should know. About eight years old, black, and dressed in jeans and a striped long-sleeved jersey, he seems very alone on this broad boulevard that runs the length of town.

He is not in school this morning like other kids his age. But very little of his life is like those of other kids his age. He doesn't know the taste of his mother's cooking because there is no place for her to cook, just a crowded, noisy cafeteria. He has no friends across the street because there is no "across the street," just redbrick remnants of industrial buildings now warehouses or offices. His bedroom has no posters or pictures on the wall, because there are no walls, just sheets hung to separate his family's area from other families'. What other children fall back on during bad times—the privacy of home, the nurture of family, the comfort of routine—are luxuries he's never known. They come to him only in dreams, as other boys dream of castles and kingdoms.

Walking with me along the same street but in the opposite direction is Drew Buscareno, in sport coat and tie, six feet tall and with shoulders square as a barn door. He sees something wrong with this picture. This child can only be on the sidewalk at this hour in this neighborhood for one reason. He has wandered away from the Center for the Homeless down the block, the center that Drew has run for the last three years. Drew turns and asks him where he's going but gets no response. He asks him his name. The boy says, "Steve." Drew takes Steve's hand and we walk to the center to find someone on staff to help.

Drew is eager to take me on a tour of the facility. We visit the area called "transitional," set aside for those who have worked, saved money, and followed the rules long enough to earn one of twelve semi-private rooms.

The other single men, nearly two hundred of them (as well as twenty-three families and sixty children), bunk in rooms stacked three cots to the ceiling, fifteen to eighteen in all, with team leaders trained in the conflict resolution skills necessary in such close and troubled quarters. For someone whose life has seesawed between bad breaks and bad choices, it seems like the last place you'd be able to sort out your problems. Its saving grace is that it is the next to last. The streets are worse.

We walk through one dorm where an older man who overslept is sitting shirtless on a folding chair pulling on his shoes and socks. He's large, with a full head of thick hair. His once barrel chest has gone fleshy and white, and he looks vulnerable sitting there, like a fish tossed onto the deck of a boat. He seems lost in thought, as if piecing together how he ended up here.

The length of stay at the center is supposed to be no more than thirty days, but that is dictated by zoning ordinances urged by fearful neighbors rather than by what social workers know is needed to help people turn their lives around. In reality many guests are here for nine months or more. "The first day is the hardest," Drew explains. "People on the streets live in survival mode. They basically live out of their brain stem. That's where the fight-or-flight impulse is housed. The brain stem controls your automatic systems, like your breathing and heart rate, and your defenses. The brain stem is a very hard place to live. The cortex is where you think, where you can reason. We help our guests understand how their brain functions, and also how their neurotransmitters function under drugs and alcohol. Our work here is geared toward 'How do you get to the cortex?' We want them to live in their cortex, not their brain stem."

The center's services are so state-of-the-art that it has become a national "market leader" in how a community deals with homelessness. That's why every recent secretary of housing and numerous policy makers and nonprofit leaders have visited or asked the center's staff to visit them.

But that's not why I went. I went because I could imagine what it's cost Drew to devote the best years of his life to an organization that will never be able to pay him what he's worth. Or what it's cost Drew to be tethered to a beeper constantly calling him back to the shelter because of a fight, or a broken window, or a broken heart. Or what it's cost Drew to work at the vortex of so much anguish that the small victories of helping someone take a step forward are dwarfed by the number of those on the waiting list.

In his late twenties, when most of his contemporaries were looking for stock options and signing bonuses, Drew chose this for a career. Now he's thirty-two with his first child on the way. If this South Bend community were a bank, Drew would be the rare customer who always makes deposits but never withdrawals, who receives no dividends other than a good conscience as his only sure reward.

IV

Acts of Conscience Occur Every Day and All Around Us

If I had the remaking of man, he wouldn't have any conscience. It is one of the most disagreeable things connected with a person; and although it certainly does a great deal of good, it cannot be said to pay, in the long run; it would be much better to have less good and more comfort. . . .I have noticed my conscience for many years, and I know it is more trouble and bother to me than anything else I started with. I suppose that in the beginning I prized it, because we prize anything that is ours; and yet how foolish it was to think so. If we look at it in another way, we see how absurd it is: if I had an anvil in me would I prize it? Of course not. And yet when you come to think, there is no real difference between a conscience and an anvil—I mean for comfort. I have noticed it a thousand times. And you could dissolve an anvil with acids, when you couldn't stand it any longer; but there isn't any way that you can work off a conscience—at least so it will stay worked off; not that I know of, anyway.

—MARK TWAIN,
A Connecticut Yankee in King Arthur's Court

WHAT WOULD I HAVE DONE?

MARCH 2003 IS the first time I've seen Goose Rocks with snow. Piled high alongside every road and atop cars that look as if they haven't been moved for months. Even the marshes, through which deep channels carry the tide inland from the ocean, are blanketed white and frozen. Huge blocks of jagged ice lie tilted on the banks as if they lost control rounding a curve and went careening out of the water.

Unlike in summer, there are no fishing boats to be seen on the horizon, no screeching calls to be heard from the gulls that usually trail them. The "Closed" sign hangs in the window of the general store as it does for forty-four weeks every year. The clam shacks that dot the roads leading into town are abandoned. The wide expanse of beach is barren. No blankets or lounge chairs. Some of the homes have boarded their picture windows. The streets are empty. The roads are clean because the snow has been plowed but it is under no pressure to melt. I see now that the solitude I enjoy here in summer is an illusion compared to this. The last days of winter are what it really means to be alone.

A few times a day someone walks past on the beach, perhaps with a dog. The person is likely wearing a hooded sweatshirt or heavy parka swelled by the wind. The body hunches into the wind, each step an extra effort. Against the sparkling sea the figure looks miniature. It is too distant to make out the person's features, or age, or even if it is a man or a woman. There is only one adjective that can possibly be applied: solitary.

That is precisely the adjective for which I've journeyed five hundred miles. Solitude is as essential to writing about conscience as to finding it. It is the one trait shared by virtually all the people described below. At some critical point they found themselves alone. Alone with an action only they could take. Perhaps more alone after taking it. Literally cut off from others, perhaps by house arrest, perhaps by their chosen form of protest, perhaps by the danger of their task that made company impossible. They were not just metaphorically, but also physically, alone.

These are the acts of conscience that have had historical or contemporary consequences and public recognition. They are the ones taught in schools, written about in books and newspapers, and referred to in obituaries forty years after the fact.

Some of these acts played a pivotal role in catalyzing or changing public opinion about issues like civil rights or Vietnam or Watergate and triggered widespread change. Others were taken at great personal risk to reputation, career, or even life and limb. They are the kind of acts we read about and stop to think: What would I have done in the same circumstances? Would I have risen to the occasion? Or would it have proven to be one of "the moments you don't get back"?

For several years now I've been finding and saving articles about such acts of conscience, an odd assortment—tales of sorrow that would not fade, of injustice that cried out for redress, of the courage to say or do what no one else was willing to say or do.

They are a diverse, occasionally obscure, but always fascinating set of stories. There is an *Economist* obituary of Alan de Lastic, archbishop of Delhi, whose photo caption describes him as "India's conscience" for his lifelong effort to protect the Christian minority from Hindu and Muslim persecution. There is the account of the murder trial of Bobby Frank Cherry for the bombing thirty-eight years ago of a Birmingham, Alabama, church in which four young black girls died. There is an article from the *New York Times* "Metro" section about the history of fasting, its power in bringing about social change, and how it is being employed in New York to protest low wages and abuse in the workplace. A sports section feature offers a remembrance of Muhammad Ali's election of conscientious objector status during the Vietnam War. And yet another *Economist* obituary praises Léopold Senghor as "the conscience of Africa" because when he stepped down as president of Senegal in 1980, he was the first leader of a modern African nation to retire voluntarily. Each is the story of taking a stand that had not been taken before, of weathering the resulting controversy, of the long and often lonely effort to achieve a just result.

There are hundreds of articles that illustrate how ubiquitous are such acts, affecting not just matters of state and world affairs but also sports, literature, business, war, and philanthropy. Ultimately they change lives, confer or constrain liberty, bestow or diminish health, make the difference in whether a child suffers or thrives, whether a nation lives in peace or war.

Acts of conscience are not academic, not something to be found in history books or by scouring the archives. They are a compelling presence in our daily lives. The more attuned we are to how often they present themselves, the more likely we are to capitalize on the opportunities they afford. The stories are legion. The ones you'll find below are just a handful, selected to illustrate their diversity and ubiquity.

INTIMATE GESTURES

IT WAS THE gentlest and most intimate of gestures: a hand on another man's shoulder. Not a word spoken. Not a shot fired. And yet it changed America.

In 1947, Brooklyn Dodgers president and general manager Branch Rickey brought Jackie Robinson up from Montreal to play with the Dodgers. This purposeful effort to integrate major league baseball predated the 1954 Supreme Court *Brown* v. *Board of Education* decision, the 1955 Montgomery bus boycott, and congressional passage of the Civil

Rights Act of 1964. It was not well received. Following one exhibition series in which Robinson batted a remarkable .515, half a dozen of his future teammates signed a petition threatening not to play if he were allowed to join the Dodgers. They were shocked when one of their teammates, shortstop Pee Wee Reese, a southerner, refused to sign.

The fans were also less than welcoming. Black cats were released onto the field; some teammates rubbed Robinson's head for good luck, while others attempted to spike him, spat tobacco juice in his face, and used racial slurs at every opportunity. Off the field, he dealt with death threats, "Dear Nigger" letters, and segregated public accommodations.

Each trip to a different ballfield became another ordeal to be faced. During a particularly difficult moment at Crosley Field in Cincinnati, as the vulgar epithets and abuse hailed down on Robinson, Pee Wee Reese, who had replaced Leo Durocher as shortstop for the Dodgers in 1940, quieted the fans and brought the entire team together by the simple gesture of walking over to second base and placing his hand on Robinson's shoulder. "That gesture spoke volumes," said teammate Carl Erskine. "Jackie Robinson—and more than that—the history of baseball had changed."

Years later, Reese recalled his reaction when he first learned that Robinson might be a teammate: "I don't know this Robinson, but I can imagine how he feels. I mean if they said to me 'Reese, you got to go over and play in the colored guys' league' how would I feel? Scared. The only white.

Lonely. But I'm a good shortstop and that's what I'd want them to see. Not my color. Just that I can play the game. And that's how I've got to look at Robinson."

With his entry into the major leagues eased by Reese, Jackie Robinson went on to become one of baseball's greats. Named to six all-star teams, he helped the Dodgers win six National League pennants and their first World Series championship, in 1955. He ranked in the top five of every major offensive category except home runs and walks. His presence was felt off the field as well. As the sportswriter Red Smith recalled the day after Jackie Robinson died: "He fought for the black man's right to a place in the white community, and he never lost sight of that goal. After he left baseball, almost everything he did was directed toward that goal. He was involved in the foundation of Freedom National Banks. He tried to get an insurance company started with black capital, and when he died he was head of a construction company building housing for blacks."

Jackie Robinson was destined for greatness by his own natural talent and indomitable will. But sometimes a helping hand brings the rendezvous with destiny sooner rather than later. In 1947 that hand belonged to Pee Wee Reese.

Born in Kentucky, Harold Henry Reese quit his job as a cable splicer for the telephone company at age eighteen to play in the minor leagues, and was sold to the Dodgers two years later in 1937. Eighteen years of dependable clutch hitting and solid defense got this former Dodger captain elected to the Hall of Fame in 1984. But his more lasting achievement was his role in the integration of baseball.

Pee Wee Reese was not a civil rights leader or activist. He didn't give speeches or appear at protest rallies. He was a shortstop, small in stature (thus the nickname), but with common decency that cast a tall shadow. Placing his hand on Jackie Robinson's shoulder on that hot summer's day may have been motivated by sympathy, solidarity, or both. It was primarily personal, yet with the most profound public consequence. He changed the way people think about race, their own prejudices, and themselves.

Pee Wee Reese teamed with Jackie Robinson for ten years. He died in 1999 at the age of eighty-one.

SOMETHING EVERYONE CAN DO

IN AUSTIN, Steven Tomlinson teaches in the MBA program at the University of Texas. He is a slight man with thin hair and protruding eyes, and a curious nature that makes him hard not to like.

At a conference we talked about writing and I told him I was trying to finish a book about how acts of conscience can change the world. I used the example of Pee Wee Reese's supportive pat on the back for Jackie Robinson, emphasizing the powerful impact it had on the fans as well as on his fellow players. He asked one of the best questions I'd encountered: "What do you think made it so powerful?"

He asked it the way a child asks a question whose answer seems obvious right up until the moment you hear it asked out loud. That's when you realize you've always taken the answer for granted and never dived deep enough below the surface. His question went to the core of what the book should be about. I was embarrassed to admit to myself not that I hadn't thought about it, but that I hadn't been thoughtful about it. I had accepted but not dissected the power of the act.

I began with the standard reply: "It was unquestionably authentic. The spontaneity of the moment guaranteed that. It showed what Pee Wee Reese was really like. And he had no ulterior motive for his action. It had all the markings of a man just trying to do the right thing, and its simplicity made its goodness unambiguous."

Tomlinson listened quietly, staring intently, not saying another word. Maybe his instinct as a teacher was that I needed to work this out on my own, that he shouldn't interrupt a train of thought, especially one that took so long to pull out of the station.

"Given the attitudes of the fans as well as his own teammates, it was also courageous," I continued. "After all, Pee Wee Reese was a southerner. From Kentucky. And he didn't see himself as any kind of activist or civil rights champion. Just a guy trying to be decent to another guy."

Finally I started to warm to the task: "But most important of all, it was something that everyone could do. In that way it not only stunned but also shamed the thousands of observers. It made them feel uncomfortable with the way they were and therefore made them want to be a different way. For that same reason, because it was something they could do too, it also empowered them."

Tomlinson's inquiry also carried the seed of a second question. I think he was asking: "Hadn't your book better give people the tools they need so that they too can act in such a manner?" It's not enough to imitate acts of conscience if you find yourself in a similar situation. It would be more valuable to have the ingredients.

ACTS OF CONSCIENCE CAN BE AS LONELY AS GOOSE ROCKS IN WINTER

ON DECEMBER 10, 1997, twenty-three-year-old Julia Butterfly Hill climbed 180 feet up an ancient redwood tree she called Luna and lived there for two years and eight days, ending her tree-sitting protest only after reaching an agreement with the Maxxam Corporation / Pacific Lumber Company, the landowner, to permanently protect the tree from logging. She had vowed "my feet would not touch the ground until I had done everything in my power to make the world aware of this problem and to stop the destruction." She endured the stormiest, coldest winter in northern California's recorded history and withstood harassment by company security wielding all-night spotlights and bullhorns. And she survived buffeting by a giant logging helicopter hovering close overhead in an attempt to drive her down with wind blasts over a hundred miles an hour. Visitors to her treetop platform included not only reporters but singers Bonnie Raitt and Joan Baez. "The first thing I came across that I could do," explained Hill, "was sit in a tree. If nothing else, my body could gain a reprieve for an over-one-thousand-year-old redwood tree."

President Nixon appointed Elliot Richardson attorney general of the United States. The Senate insisted, as part of the confirmation process, that Richardson appoint a special prosecutor to investigate the escalating Watergate scandal. His choice was Archibald Cox, a former law student of his. At the time of his appointment, Richardson had been serving as secretary of defense. He had also been appointed by Nixon during his first term to be secretary of health, education and welfare, and undersecretary of state. As President Nixon's troubles began to destroy his presidency, Richardson sought to avoid a direct confrontation with the man who had three times invited him to be a member of his administration. But when Nixon ordered him to fire Cox in reaction to Cox's efforts to force release of the White House tapes, Richardson felt that he had no choice but to resign on principle rather than carry out such an order. His deputy attorney general, William Ruckelshaus, was fired by Nixon after he too refused to fire Cox. The resulting firestorm eventually led to impeachment hearings and the resignation of the president for the first time in American history.

Another resignation based on principle was that of Secretary of State Cyrus Vance, who resigned to protest President Carter's decision to try to free Americans held hostage in Iran through the use of military force. (Vance was one of only three secretaries of state to quit over principle, the others being Lewis Cass, who quit in 1860 to protest President James Buchanan's refusal to take strong measures against the secessionists, and William Jennings Bryan, who was protesting our entry into World War I.) Vance tendered his resignation before learning of the failure of the mission, which was compromised by the collision of a rescue helicopter and a cargo plane that killed eight American servicemen. He told his subordinates that he was heartbroken he had to quit but that principle dictated he must.

Half a world away from where Julia Butterfly Hill slept on a platform at the top of a tree, another woman slept in a car, in the middle of a muddy, mosquito-infested field. Like Hill's, her actions were closely observed, especially by her adversaries. Her name is Aung San Suu Kyi and she has long led the opposition to Burma's dictatorial and ruthless government. Stopped while en route to do party organizing work, she refused government requests to return to Rangoon.

Aung San, fifty-five years old, began her struggle against Burma's military government in 1988. The military regime that seized power from the people on September 18, 1988, placed her under house arrest in Rangoon under martial law that allows for detention without charge or trial for three years. She went on a hunger strike to protect the students taken from her house to the Military Intelligence Interrogation Center, and was recognized as a prisoner of conscience by Amnesty International. Despite her continuing detention, the National League for Democracy won a landslide victory in the general election by securing 82 percent of the seats, but the military junta refused to recognize the results of the election. Aung San lived under house arrest from 1988 to 1995. In isolation, her defiance gained her fame. She was awarded the Nobel Peace Prize in 1991.

In March 2003 Aung San explained to *Parade* magazine: "As I travel through my country, people often ask me how it feels to have been imprisoned in my home—first for six years, then for nineteen months. How could I stand the separation from family and friends? It is ironic, I say, that in an authoritarian state it is only the prisoner of conscience who is genuinely free. Yes, we have given up our right to a normal life. But we have stayed true to that most precious part of our humanity—our conscience."

In June 2003, Aung San was once again taken into custody by the ruling military junta, this time triggering protests and sanctions from foreign governments around the world.

Acting on conscience can mean being as alone as a visitor to Goose Rocks in winter. Whether you are a secretary of state or a twenty-three-year-old on a journey of self-discovery, following your conscience could mean isolating yourself, being cut off from the life you have lived. It is a gamble whether acting alone in a given instance will have more impact than acting in concert with others—whether breaking away may be more important than joining together.

Such acts may require a willingness to do what is unpopular, resist entreaties to the contrary, and sacrifice both pleasure and power. But of course it is these very sacrifices and especially the aloneness that give such actions their moral authority. Just as a lighthouse derives its worth standing alone in dangerous waters, so too do these individuals stand taller for standing alone.

As my friend Jeff Swartz, CEO of Timberland, who works to integrate conscience and commerce, explained to me: "Rabbi Joseph Soloveitchik writes about the lonely person of faith needing to experience his or her absolutely solitary journey toward an individually earned redemption.

"'Even when all the roads are barred to him, there still exists somewhere a secret path that twists and turns between hills and valleys, that climbs to dizzying heights and drops to bewildering depths, and he knows that if he follows this path no one can stand in his way. Should he insist upon joining others on the main thoroughfare, he will find himself confronting a barrier. The highway is closed. . . . [N]evertheless, though the highway be blocked, it is still possible to travel the hidden byways that wind their way through the jungle. . . . The public thoroughfare does not lead man to the goal—only the solitary road.' [*On Repentance,* pp. 239–40.]

"And, by contrast, the Rav adds magnificent paragraphs about Kol Nidre night—the night, when all who travel their individual paths come together, in congregation, unified in the experience of individual searching. They remain lonely voyagers, but they are united in congregation. And in this coming together, they create something that benefits each individual—they create the power of congregation."

CONSCIENCE IS A CLOCK THAT NEVER WINDS DOWN

CONSCIENCE TICKS LIKE a clock that never needs rewinding. Its sound gets louder, not fainter, with the passage of time, as Edgar Allan Poe showed in "The Tell-Tale Heart." The weight of conscience grows heavier until the status quo can no longer sustain it. Something has to give. Action and redress become inevitable.

In 1989, a court reporter revisited a story more than a quarter of a century old and caught the interest of Bobby DeLaughter, the Hinds County, Mississippi, assistant district attorney. The investigation that followed finally led to a conviction in the 1963 killing of NAACP field secretary Medgar Evers as he returned home from a late night at work. His wife and three children watched as he crawled, mortally wounded, from his driveway to their doorstep.

Byron De La Beckwith was charged with the killing but twice acquitted. The story that caught DeLaughter's interest revealed that there might have been jury tampering in the 1964 trial. It was meeting Evers's widow, Myrlie, that convinced DeLaughter to go forward: "After meeting her and listening to her describe what had happened the night Medgar was killed, it just really sent home to me in my mind that there are some things that not only span the races but also span time as well."

DeLaughter faced great personal cost. He received death threats and was snubbed by white Mississippians, and his marriage dissolved. His autobiography makes clear that he feared there would be consequences: "I very much enjoy the courtroom and would have liked to have been a DA or, particularly, a judge. I knew right off the bat that this would be political suicide, but you've got to be able to look yourself in the mirror. I couldn't turn my back on this case and be able to do that."

In 1994 Byron De La Beckwith was convicted and sentenced to life in prison. DeLaughter's book about the trial is called *Never Too Late*. After the book's publication he was appointed a judge.

In April 2001, Birmingham brought to trial two men, Thomas Blanton, Jr., and Bobby Frank Cherry, for the September 15, 1963, bombing of a church basement that killed four girls, one aged eleven and the others all fourteen, in one of the most tragic and terrible moments of the civil rights movement. For nearly thirty-eight years, Birmingham had waited for these two suspects to face their day in court. According to *The New York Times*, "State and federal investigators were inspired to reopen the case against them in 1996 after prosecutors in other states won convictions in several dusty killings in the civil rights era."

In turn, the conviction of Cherry brought renewed attention to the unsolved slayings of James Chaney, Andrew Goodman, and Michael Schwerner, found beaten and shot in an earthen dam in Philadelphia, Mississippi, the last major unsolved atrocity of the civil rights era. As the lead prosecutor in the Bobby Frank Cherry case explained, "People can forgive and move on. The law can't forgive."

. . .

On Sunday, December 1, 2002, *The New York Times* published a story called "Emmett Till's Long Shadow: A Hate Crime That Refuses to Give Up Its Ghosts."

The article recounted the events of forty-seven years ago in which a fourteen-year-old black youth was murdered by two white men for allegedly whistling at a white woman. Emmett Till's mother, Mamie Till-Mobley, is at the heart of a new documentary film about the murder and, before her death, was also writing a book about it. Her co-author, a Chicago lawyer, explained its significance this way: "Of the thousands of lynchings that occurred since Reconstruction the one name everyone remembers is Emmett Till. It burned the race problem into our consciousness, the first international coverage, the first real media event of the modern civil rights movement. And no one ever had to pay."

In October 2001, Ireland, in only the thirteenth state funeral in the nation's history, reburied the remains of ten Irish Republican Army volunteers executed by the British during Ireland's war of independence eighty years ago. It took seven years of negotiations between government authorities and the men's families for the bodies to be exhumed from their graves in Mountjoy Jail, where they were hanged in 1920 and 1921, and re-interred closer to their families.

This action was widely seen as a long-overdue commemoration of national heroes, and Cardinal Cathal Daly suggested that "surely the state funeral can be an occasion for an examination of conscience about the ideals of the men who died and about our responsibility for translating these ideals into today's realities."

One of the most remarkable stories, which goes back far longer than eighty years, may be Pope John Paul II's March 12, 2000, sweeping apology for the errors of his church over the last two millennia. Seven cardinals and bishops stood before the Pope as, dressed in purple robes and embracing the crucifix in St. Peter's Basilica, he cited significant Catholic lapses past and present, including religious intolerance and injustice toward Jews, women, immigrants, indigenous peoples, and the poor. The Pope's public act of repentance was unprecedented in the history of the Catholic Church.

"Recognizing the deviances of the past serves to reawaken our consciences to the compromises of the present," said the pontiff. In past years the Pope had said repeatedly that the new evangelization he called for in the third millennium could take place only after a church-wide "purification of memory."

There are many stories about the compelling need to redress grievances no matter how long ago they occurred. The need comes not from political pressure or external force, but invariably from that small voice within. Sometimes its flame has flickered or burned in only a single heart, but one conscience is enough to keep it alive.

CONSCIENCE TAKES COURAGE

"WHAT'S ESSENTIAL IS invisible to the eye," wrote Saint-Exupéry in *The Little Prince*. The words echo as I turn to look back at the nondescript townhouse on O Street near Dupont Circle that keeps alive the memory of one of the most remarkable acts of conscience in modern history.

There were many witnesses to the Holocaust who also played a role in exposing and ending it, but perhaps one of the most courageous was Jan Karski, who made it his job to inform Anthony Eden, Franklin Roosevelt, and other Allied leaders in 1942 of the Nazi extermination camps, and to give them a detailed account of the systematic slaughter of the Jews.

In the late summer of 1942, Karski, a twenty-eight-year-old diplomat for the Polish government in exile, was approached by two members of the Jewish underground who had briefly left the Warsaw Ghetto and wanted to make the world aware of the extermination of the Jews. In August of that year he entered the cellar of an apartment house on the Aryan side of the Ghetto wall and crawled through a tunnel, emerging in ragged clothes and a Star of David armband to see for himself the crowded tenements and the hungry and dying Jews. A second risky fact-finding mission had him donning the uniform of a Ukrainian militiaman and entering

Izbica, a small town near Warsaw that was home to a concentration camp, where he witnessed Jews being attacked and herded into boxcars.

Karski escaped through Berlin, then Vichy France, then Spain, where a rendezvous led to a passage to Gibraltar and then London. There he turned over microfilm documenting resistance activity and informing British foreign secretary Anthony Eden of the destruction of the Jews. In July 1943 he arrived in the United States. He told *The New York Times*: "Almost every individual was sympathetic to my reports concerning the Jews. But when I reported to the leaders of governments, they discarded their conscience, their personal feeling. . . . The war strategy was the military defeat of Germany and the defeat of Germany's war potential for all eternity. Nothing could interfere with the military crushing of the Third Reich."

Though Karski was almost my neighbor, worshiping at the Polish church in Silver Spring, I knew little of him until I read his obituary in 2001. But that was my own fault. For nearly thirty years after the war he was a professor at Georgetown University and well known to the sizable diplomatic community that makes Washington its home.

As I searched the Internet for more information, I came across a link to something called the Jan Karski Room, housed within the American Center of Polish Culture. The address was 2025 O Street in Washington, D.C., just a short drive from my office. I asked my assistant, Chuck Scofield, to call and find out their hours and how we could visit. The only response he got was a recording by one of those disembodied voices saying, "You have reached 202 . . ."

We decided to take our chances. Our taxi took us to a quiet residential street. A lace curtain made it hard to see inside, but the house looked dark and empty. We buzzed the intercom. A small woman with bobbed blond hair, glasses, and a blue sweater looked at us curiously and then opened wide the door to one of the least known treasures of art, culture, and history in the nation's capital.

"We were wondering if we could see the Jan Karski Room," I said.

"Yes, sure," the woman replied. Her name was Anna, and the deliberate but timid way she carried herself made her look even smaller than she actually was.

The Karski Room is a replica of the home study of this brave soldier and professor. "Everything is authentic," Anna assured us. "His desk, chairs, sofa, the books, the pens and pencils. And here you can touch. These things you can pick up. It is okay." The walls are covered with testimonials, photos, and awards.

The household items left by Karski are unremarkable, mostly because mere objects cannot convey life as Karski lived it. In 1940, having been caught by the Gestapo and tortured mercilessly for three days, Karski feared he might crack and betray his colleagues, so he withdrew a razor blade from a secret compartment in his boot heel and cut his own wrists. "I have little tolerance for pain," he once explained to his Georgetown students. The suicide failed, and eventually he escaped from the hospital. It was after this that he'd agreed to don rags and be smuggled twice into the Warsaw Ghetto, and then later to visit Izbica, the sorting point for the Belzec concentration camp, where the Nazis murdered 600,000 Jews and others.

By July 1943, Karski had made his way to the United States, hoping to redress what he saw as "too much indifference, self-interest, self-imposed disbelief in allied nations." To facilitate his meeting with President Roosevelt, Karski met first with Supreme Court Justice Felix Frankfurter. The justice's response to what Karski told him was "A man like me speaking to a man like you must be totally frank. So I must say, I am unable to believe you."

The Polish ambassador who had accompanied Karski to the meeting was shocked. "Felix, you don't mean it. How can you call him a liar to his face? The authority of my government is behind him. You know who he is."

"Mr. Ambassador, I did not say the man is lying. I said I am unable to believe him. There is a difference," replied Frankfurter.

Nevertheless, Karski did eventually see Roosevelt. As a result, the president established the War Refugee Board to help settle surviving Jews. The mission, according to John Pehle, who led it, "changed U.S. policy overnight from indifference to affirmative action." In 1994 Karski was made an honorary citizen of the state of Israel, and he was nominated in 1998 for the Nobel Peace Prize by the Holocaust Museum in Jerusalem.

"Take your time," Anna says, as we linger in the room. There are many photos on the walls. It is impossible to find one in which Karski, tall and gaunt, is not immaculately tailored in a fine suit. In picture after picture, those posing with him at dinners or events, pleased to be in the presence of such a man, smile for the camera. Karski rarely does. He is looking down, or away, a far-off look in his eyes.

It is a large house, and except for the three of us, it is empty, as I suspect it almost always is.

"Do visitors come to see this room very often?" I ask.

"Every once in a while," she replies softly, unconvincingly.

If you seek solitude among the crowds of tourists that throng Washington, you can find it in the Jan Karski Room on O Street. It is fitting that this should be a place not well trafficked. After all, Karski's ambition was not to publicly lead others, but to privately listen and remain true to his own small voice within. And while he lived a long life surrounded by countrymen, admirers, students, and friends, he could not have escaped the awful solitude that comes with having borne witness to something so terrible and extraordinary that even his most impassioned pleas could not bring the likes of Felix Frankfurter to believe it.

Karski was a devout and lifelong Catholic. He once explained: "My faith tells me that the second original sin has been committed by humanity through commission or omission, or self-imposed ignorance, or insensitivity, or hypocrisy, or heartless rationalization. That sin will haunt humanity to the end of time. It does haunt me, and I want it to be so."

In a city of colossal marble monuments, to Lincoln, Washington, Jefferson, and recently Franklin Roosevelt as well, the artifacts of Jan Karski's study seem unremarkable as a memorial. But these small items are not without grand purpose. Even a slender thread can keep us linked to the essential, though less visible, lessons of our past. This room that houses them reminds us that even the most ordinary of us, those who leave behind not grand temples but only a chair, desk, and pens and pencils, are yet capable of the extraordinary impact that abiding one's conscience will achieve.

On March 16, 1968, Herbert L. Carter refused to obey Lt. William Calley's order to shoot defenseless Vietnamese villagers at My Lai. The official army account was that the America Division's 11th Brigade infantrymen from Task Force Barker had raided a Vietcong stronghold, killing 128 enemy in a running battle. But Carter testified that "there was no resistance from the village. There was no armed enemy in the village," and went on to describe the atrocities in graphic detail before the U.S Army's Criminal Investigation Division. More than five hundred unarmed Vietnamese civilians had been massacred in all.

On that morning, twenty-four-year-old Hugh Thompson was flying a helicopter low over the village and saw what was happening. He landed his chopper between the troops and the shelter where Vietnamese women and children had taken cover. He told his crewmates that if the Americans fired on the civilians, they should shoot them. In 1998 he received the Pentagon's Soldiers Medal. Lieutenant Calley was sentenced to life in prison and served three years.

Thompson explained years later that "the things that went wrong that day were poor leadership, peer pressure, and prejudice." It was a remarkably concise summary of virtually every facet of conscience: the need to be true to  oneself rather than succumb to peer pressure; the power of leading from within, not following others; the need to see and learn and witness for oneself rather than to prejudge.

Even though we expect the worst from war, we also expect the worst to stop somewhere short of violating our conscience.

SINS OF OMISSION

"WHY DON'T WE get a movie?" Zach suggested casually on the ride back to the house one day after a hockey tournament. "It's been a while since we've done that."

"Sure, pal, what would you like to see?"

"Let's get *Les Mis,*" he proposed.

"*Les Mis?*" I looked over at him, not sure I had heard right.

"Yeah, not the musical, the other one."

I couldn't have been more surprised. Astonished, actually. Zach's taste in film runs more to *Die Hard* and *Terminator II* than to French classics, more to John Candy than Jean Valjean.

I rushed to the video store before he could change his mind. Unlike his repeated viewings of *The Mummy Returns,* this was something we could watch together. We both enjoyed it. Liam Neeson and Geoffrey Rush turned in strong performances, and Zach asked a few questions about the French Revolution. It seemed he was maturing, developing an appreciation for the finer things, perhaps even a passion for social justice.

The rest of the weekend was so lazy and relaxed that when I drove Zach to school Monday morning I wondered whether he had finished all of his homework. He insisted he had. I was careful to ask the question several other ways. He has a knack for exploiting linguistic loopholes that would make a certain ex-president proud.

"You're caught up in every class?" I pressed.

"Sure am, Pops."

"No papers due?"

"Nope."

English is the subject he's lagged in a bit during this tenth-grade year, so I asked him to show me what they were reading. He didn't say anything but instead reached into the bulky backpack resting on his lap and after a few minutes of rummaging through it produced a brand-new copy of Victor Hugo's *Les Misérables*. It had no more been opened than if it were owned by George W. Bush himself. He held it toward me, but said nothing, maintaining a studied casualness.

I felt the way a losing chess player must feel, not when defeat comes, but when the realization dawns that defeat came three moves ago. When a teenager appears to be acting out of character, this is usually a signal of just the opposite—that he has reverted to precisely the true character you've suspected all along. Prison wardens recognize such behavior as a precursor of trouble. Parents, lacking sufficient experience, or cynicism, are easier marks.

I gave Zach a sidelong glance indicating my disapproval. He countered with the wounded expression of the unjustly accused. This pivot from defendant to victim was smooth and seamless. I found myself almost admiring it, at least in terms of craft. He'd had plenty of opportunity to practice over the years.

I didn't want to make too big a deal of it. Zach hadn't told a lie when he asked to rent *Les Mis*. In fact, with the challenging years of middle school behind him, he'd all but given up outright lying. It's impossible to know whether this was a consequence of character development or of having been caught so many times, but after having heard my share of whoppers over the years, I viewed this as a major step forward. From his perspective, however, it was such a significant sacrifice that little more should be expected of him—an interesting approach to managing expectations!

Truth telling is an acquired behavior. It doesn't come naturally to children. From the time we are schooled in George Washington's "I cannot tell a lie" myth about chopping down the cherry tree, the wrong-versus-right view of lying is drawn in black-and-white terms, clearly discernible even to a child. But life more often confronts us with shades of gray. Sins of omission. Cutting corners. Mitigating circumstances. The temptation to allow a false perception to stand. Unlike lies, which we know are wrong, sins of omission lend themselves to long internal debate aimed at rationalization. 

In the grand scheme of things, watching a video of *Les Mis* was nothing more than a classic student shortcut, CliffsNotes à la Blockbuster. But Zach's omission had been not only convenient but purposeful. It seemed as good a time as any to discuss how often such opportunities present themselves among life's choices, to assess where they rank on the relief map of slippery slopes and how likely the truth is to rise to the surface eventually anyway. He didn't give much ground, and I hadn't expected him to. But a moment of uncertainty had flashed across his face, an unspoken questioning or self-doubt. As one who takes small victories where he finds them, I seized on this as civilization's leap forward for the day.

This happened to be the same weekend that all of the political talk shows were consumed with another omission, of considerably more consequence, regarding former senator Bob Kerrey's role in the events of thirty-two years ago when as many as a dozen women and children were killed by his SEAL team. It is a fascinating example of what conscience can repress and also ultimately reveal. Kerrey's wasn't an act of conscience so much as a clearing of one, and not principally a voluntary one at that.

In 1990 I traveled to Vietnam with then Senator Kerrey and a small group that included a SEAL team colleague of his; a Marine; James Webb, a Vietnam veteran who also served as secretary of the navy; and a few reporters. It was Kerrey's first trip back since he'd lost his right leg in a firefight and been evacuated twenty-five years earlier. The United States was moving in the direction of normalizing relations with Vietnam, and it was believed that this trip and the discussions to be held there could move things forward. We returned again a year later.

Bob Kerrey and I met during the 1984 presidential campaign, when I worked for Senator Gary Hart, the dark horse running against establishment front-runner Walter Mondale. Bob, who'd made a career out of bucking conventional wisdom, was the only Democratic governor to endorse Hart in the Democratic primaries. He led our winning campaign in Nebraska, and also lent star power, including that of Debra Winger, his girlfriend at the time, to our fund-raising efforts in other places.

We stayed in touch only intermittently after Hart lost and Bob left the governor's office in 1986. In 1987, Bob's respite was interrupted by the sudden death of Nebraska's senator Ed Zorinsky.

Late one afternoon I got a call from Omaha. It was Bob's scheduler, Cindy Dwyer, asking if I could pick Bob up at National Airport at eleven o'clock that night, and would I mind bringing him a fresh shirt and toothbrush.

Just before midnight, on one of those now-long-gone innocent evenings when you could leave your car running in the passenger arrival lane of the airport terminal, Bob leaped into the front seat of my car. "I'll get right to the point," he said. "My national finance director has come down with leukemia and I'd like you to take his place."

I wanted to work with Bob, but not for him. I didn't want to be solely dependent on any politician again. I'd had a taste of independence for a few short months and found that I valued it more than breakfast in the senators' dining room, more than riding in Secret Service limousines, more even than the steady salary that a government job offers. I agreed to do the job as a volunteer, commuting to Omaha for the next year for plane fare only.

Bob won his race. We had breakfast the next morning, and before I knew it I had a U.S. Senate ID hanging around my neck again.

Never having served in the military, let alone in a war, I can still remember how self-conscious and inadequate I felt in the company of the group traveling to Vietnam. I couldn't imagine what I would have to offer as they relived some of the experiences that must have been the most profound of their lives. But there were no war stories, certainly no machismo or swaggering, nor was there much in the way of the raw emotions that I anticipated might be triggered by the trip. In fact much was left unsaid. I got the distinct impression that despite this return journey there were places and times they could not get back to and dared not try. They seemed as vulnerable and as unsure of themselves as they must have felt in the jungle when barely out of their teens.

I was chief of staff in Kerrey's Senate office, and because he was new to Washington and single at the time, we went to dinner together almost every night after the Senate recessed for the evening. As close as we were, as much as we talked about, there was always a wall that came up about Vietnam, a certain distance that was hard to breach. The part of his life that he was best known for was the part I knew least about.

Until the world learned of it, I was not aware of Kerrey's role in the events at Thanh Phong or of the anguish he's carried all these years. I have since tried repeatedly to close my eyes, put myself in his shoes, and imagine the horror he must have felt when he learned of the consequences of his actions. It's a revealing exercise. My eyes don't stay closed for very long, nor do I stay in his shoes long. It is truly unimaginable, in the literal sense of the word. But it has given me some small sense of how and why he has kept that experience at bay.

CONSCIENCE AT WORK AND PLAY

ON APRIL 28, 1967, heavyweight boxing champ Muhammad Ali refused induction into military service, claiming conscientious objector status and affirming his opposition to the war in Vietnam.

Three years earlier, on the day after he defeated the heavily favored Sonny Liston to win his first heavyweight championship, Ali had changed his name from Cassius Clay and converted to the Nation of Islam. His words to a roomful of reporters in response to a question about whether he was "a card-carrying Black Muslim" forever changed the world of sports: "'Card-carrying'—what does that mean? I believe in Allah and I believe in peace. . . . I don't have to be what you want me to be. I'm free to be what I want." As David Remnick, editor of *The New Yorker* and author of *King of the World: Muhammad Ali and the Rise of an American Hero,* explained, "He had forsaken the image of the unthreatening black fighter established by Joe Louis and then imitated by Jersey Joe Walcott, and Floyd Patterson, and dozens of others. Clay was declaring that he would not fit any stereotypes not of his own making."

When Ali's draft notice came, his words were even more provocative and set off a firestorm of condemnation. "I ain't got no quarrel with them Vietcong. No Vietcong ever called me a nigger." He was immediately denounced by all the major sportswriters, including Red Smith, who wrote: "Cassius makes himself as sorry a spectacle as those unwashed punks who picket and demonstrate against the war."

Within minutes of his induction refusal, the New York State Athletic Commission stripped Ali of his title, declaring his actions "detrimental to the best interests of boxing." He was convicted of draft evasion and sentenced to five years in prison. The Supreme Court overturned the conviction, but during four years of internal exile, Ali lost millions of dollars and the peak years of his career. Through it all, he declared, "My principles are more important than my money or my title."

With time, the columnists changed and Ali's opposition to the war became a more widely shared position. Ali's example helped inspire Dr. Martin Luther King, Jr.—who had been reluctant to alienate the Johnson administration and its support of the civil rights agenda—to voice his own opposition to the war for the first time. Ali was also cited by Arthur Ashe, Billie Jean King, and others as they fought their own battles to change the face of sports and society. As Max Wallace wrote in *The New York Times,* chronicling Ali's legacy of principle over profits: "It is time to measure athletes for more than just their athletic accomplishments and to hold them accountable for their behavior outside the arena, to recognize their significant impact on a large segment of society. Today's generation needs sports heroes whose principles and aspirations extend beyond the next pair of Air Nikes."

. . .

Human dramas rather than sports feats often dominate coverage of the Olympics. That may be more true than ever of the Salt Lake City Games of 2002, which will be remembered less for the skill of the skiers and the speed of the luge than for the irrepressible force of one misguided woman's tormented conscience.

Pre-game hype predictably focused on training regimens, drug testing, and athletes who overcame long odds. But once the games commenced, the spotlight turned out to be not on some long-simmering competition between two Olympians at the top of their game, but on a conflict between one woman at the top of her profession and her own conscience. The woman was French ice skating judge Marie-Reine Le Gougne, traumatized by her complicity in a vote-swapping scheme between French and Russian judges.

As *The New York Times* reported on Sunday, February 18, 2002, the biggest judging scandal in the history of the winter Olympics unraveled at a standard post-competition judges' review of the controversial decision. Just moments after the head referee handed each judge a piece of paper with a passage about honesty and integrity, "the judge Marie-Reine Le Gougne began to sob, officials said. . . . 'I hadn't asked her a question . . . it was an outburst,'" according to the head referee. The story continued. "For several minutes the wail from Le Gougne grew so loud that one official said a person in the room stripped tape over the crack in the door in an apparent soundproofing effort. . . . No one embraced Le Gougne, the stylish 40-year-old Frenchwoman, as she cried out. . . . They already knew why Le Gougne was distraught, they said: her conscience had caught up with her."

The photographs of Le Gougne portray an attractive, elegant woman, almost regal in bearing, sitting beside the rink, seemingly confident and at peace with her judgments. But the elegance masks what must have been a grueling ascension to judging at the Olympic level: relentless travel, long hours at cold ice rinks that all look alike right down to the advertisements painted on the surrounding white boards, countless early mornings warming hands around paper cups of steaming coffee with no one else except perhaps the skaters' families watching. Such a journey to the Olympic Village requires a passport stamped *competence, standards, reputation*. Le Gougne wasn't sobbing because she had betrayed the International Skating Union, but because she had betrayed herself.

Her tears confessed what her words would not, her pain so palpable as to be physical. That's not uncommon. Novelist Ward Just wrote in a short story called "Cease-Fire" about a man who fell seriously ill when his actions betrayed his principles: "Everyone knows that my sort of disorder does not arise from an unhappy childhood or some long buried trauma, nor is it revealed in nighttime dreams or nightmares. Still less is it corrected by the self-administered caress. It rises from the collision between one's public and private selves. It is an accident of history this head-on crash, and naturally there is noise and confusion and injury as in any accident."

The *New York Times* story concluded that "if Le Gougne had not wept, if she had remained stony faced throughout the past week, no one would have suspected the Russian gold was anything more than a hotly debated finish created by judges with questionable tastes." Le Gougne had not been alone in her scoring. Two other judges scored the same way. She was alone only in her reasoning. In the end her conscience proved to be stronger than her nationalism.

The Olympic Games not only entertain but also inspire. That is part of the justification for the enormous attention and expense on behalf of what are, as their name says, only games. The gold medalists almost always embody more than technical superiority, rigorous training, endurance, and strength. There is some additional quality that gives them a winner's edge. And I don't mean steroids. It's a certain largeness of spirit, a fullness of heart, a unity of mind and body and spirit that makes them unbeatable. Judges perform no better than athletes when that unity fissures and cracks. Marie-Reine Le Gougne learned that lesson when she raised wrestling with conscience to the level of an Olympic sport, and lost.

Legendary jockey Chris Antley died at thirty-four. He suffered from depression and alcohol and drug abuse, a cocaine user from the age of twenty-two. He once won nine races in a single day and rode one winner for a record sixty-four consecutive days. During an improbable career that began at age fourteen in Elloree, South Carolina, he won 3,500 races, many of which were long shots.

The Economist wrote that "the most famous was Charismatic, a lightly regarded horse Mr. Antley rode to victory in the 1999 Derby and the Preakness, the first two prongs of America's triple crown. It was in losing the third, the Belmont Stakes, that he became a legend. At the finish, Charismatic stumbled. Rather than push him across the line, Mr. Antley jumped off, settling for third place, and cradled Charismatic's shattered leg, saving the horse's life."

Antley did capture national attention that day, and deservedly so, but not because he decided against pushing his horse across the line. What actually happened is a little more complicated than *The Economist*'s summary.

It was June 5, 1999, and a record Belmont crowd. It was near the wire, at the eighth-mile pole, that Antley felt the beautiful chestnut colt break down. "There was a different rhythm," he said afterward with tears streaming down his face. But it was only after he crossed the finish line, not before, that he tried to pull Charismatic to a stop. Sixty yards past the wire he bailed, falling as he hit the ground. He scrambled to his feet, and standing in harm's way by the horse's side, picked up the injured leg, holding it off the ground so the colt could not put weight on it.

One of the worst sounds in the world is the silence of

85,818 people who have watched a horse break down. Cheering lustily one moment, as still as rock the next. The majesty and enormous strength of the animal combined with such helplessness rob lungs of breath and mouth of words.

In the photo taken at just that moment, while Antley gently supports the left front hoof with his left hand and holds the reins firmly under the horse's chin with his right, Charismatic looks anything but lame. His right front hoof is just a few inches off the ground and his back legs are powering a pivot. The veins in his chest and neck stand out like a relief map. Antley's cheek is against the horse's shoulder, his mouth open slightly as if saying something soothing and reassuring. A racetrack attendant in chest-protector vest with walkie-talkie clipped to his belt is also in the picture, his body crouched and tense, next to Antley, who seems completely calm.

Jumping off the horse had to have been part instinct and part conscious decision, albeit a lightning-quick one. The horse looks as surprised as anyone. In the picture his face seems to have a quizzical look, eyes focusing curiously on Antley's hands beneath his fractured leg. Veterinarians agreed this saved the horse's life. Whether it was humanly possible to act even more quickly than he did is just not known.

Antley's gift was coaxing horses to their best performance. He had no such luck with himself. Three times in the last ten years he'd entered rehab. Cocaine, alcohol, bipolar disorder. He talked often of the agony of shrinking his 145-pound frame down to the 116 pounds he needed to be to ride. *The*

Economist reported that he had to "lead a life of staggering deprivation to meet the strict weight restrictions of his trade. Not only food, but often liquid including water, was off limits. Like many jockeys he took diuretics to drain water from his system and ran up to 25 miles a day. At times his mouth was so dry he could not speak."

The only one Antley ever took it all out on was himself. He was unfailingly kind and generous to others, even while in battle with his worst demons, and his action in saving Charismatic that June day was completely in character, according to friends and family. But he could not save himself. His brother Brian found him dead in his home on December 2 of that year. The coroner diagnosed severe head trauma but declined to rule his death a homicide. His wife, Natalie Jowatt, a producer for ABC Sports, came to the funeral pregnant with their first child, a daughter.

Chris Antley was a tragic figure. But heroic as well? I'm not sure. I'd at least give him the benefit of the doubt. Acts of conscience at racetracks are few and far between, and we have to take them where we find them.

At about the same time, *The New York Times* ran a brief editorial essay about Dr. Matthew Lukwiya, the medical superintendent who died leading the battle against the Ebola outbreak in Uganda at St. Mary's Hospital in Lacor. At least 162 people in Uganda died after suffering high fevers and hemorrhages from this virus, for which there is no known treatment except containment.

Dr. Lukwiya held a master's degree from the Liverpool School of Tropical Medicine in England but had worked at Lacor since 1983. It is one of the better hospitals of sub-Saharan Africa, but not equipped to treat and control epidemics. By early December, eleven nurses, a hospital driver, and a cleaner had died of the disease. The *Times* editorial recounts "one terrible day" when three health workers died in twenty-four hours. "The nurses gathered at the hospital to protest the dangers of their job. Dr. Lukwiya addressed the meeting. 'Those who want to leave can leave,' he said. 'But as for me, I will not betray my profession.' On November 30, two days after the three health workers died, a male nurse who had taken sick and was covered in blood fell out of bed. The nurses declined to pick him up, so Dr. Lukwiya did. A short while later he had a fever." A quiet man in his early forties, Dr. Lukwiya left a wife and five children.

Matthew Lukwiya and Chris Antley. One a skilled doctor, educated and deliberate. The other often a very sick patient, a high school dropout whose torments sometimes drove him out of control. But each with his own personal definition of what it meant not to betray his profession. Both with lightning-quick reflexes that put them in harm's way and consciences that kept them there.

That each of us is capable of such acts, whether jockey, physician, or president, draws us closer to them, stimulates self-reflection, makes us ask, "What would I have done in the same situation?" Examining the acts of conscience of others becomes a way of learning more about oneself.

Not every act of conscience is so heroic as to save a life or so dangerous as to sacrifice one. There are gray areas and close calls. An individual's motivations are not always clear enough to be certain of, nor is his or her self-interest. Acts of conscience don't always reflect a lifetime's behavior. They may occur so fast that if you blinked you'd miss them. Judging acts of conscience is a subjective process that depends on one's own conscience as a reference point. Living by one's conscience doesn't mean never making mistakes. It cannot guarantee always doing the right thing. No one is that perfect. But it does permit what Socrates asked for in the prayer from *Phaedrus* when he said: "May the outward and inward man be one."

Amid the bookies and the betting windows and the handicappers, you might not expect to find a large conscience inside a diminutive, demon-driven jockey. Nor might you expect word of a quiet doctor's compassion in the remote interior of the African continent to reach a million readers of *The New York Times*. But such can be the power of a single act. Such is the grace that attends when the outward and inward man are one.

WHEN CONSCIENCE IS NOWHERE TO BE FOUND

One by one, the 11 boys sat down with police detectives to answer questions about their encounter with a homeless alcoholic who was nameless to them. . . . None used the word murder in explaining how a band of boys had beaten the man to death, ending a violent spree on the last day of school. He was homeless but he had a name, Hector Robles . . .

—*The New York Times,*
June 29, 2001

THERE ARE TIMES and places stained by the glaring absence of conscience. The corner of Jasper and Totowa Streets in Paterson, New Jersey, seemed to be one of them. It was the most mindless form of brutality, not the quick and easy carnage of gunfire, but the harder work of battering someone slowly to death with fists and feet.

Hector Robles had lived on the streets for nearly fifteen years. A quiet man, he favored a tire as his stoop. His siblings frequently checked on him. Paterson has homeless shelters, alcoholism clinics, and mental health associations, many of which were established for people just like Hector.

The New York Times ran a photo of the site where Robles was kicked and beaten. One of those shrines with notes and flowers had sprung up to compensate for everyone's ability to ignore Robles while he was alive. It was situated near the corner of a busy street, between the two old redbrick factory buildings where they say he enjoyed the quiet. The tire upon which Robles used to sit was filled with candles. Across the bricks someone had spray-painted in white letters: R.I.P. HECTOR ROBLES 1958–2001. Next to the epitaph was taped a white sheet with a photo of Robles in the middle and his name and date of death spray-painted in red. The sheet covered three quarters of an American flag that someone had hung there earlier.

Paterson's chief homicide investigator is Bill Purdy. Fifteen years on the job gives him a unique perspective on violence, gangs, homeless men and women, how we raise and protect children, and where conscience fits. Purdy's office investigates thirty to forty murders a year. "My friends say it makes me coldhearted," he said with a smile that contradicted his words.

Purdy is a compact man in a crisp white shirt and tie. He carries himself as if containing a surplus of energy that could spill over. "I'm trying to make sense of this," he said as he waved a chart matching defendants' names and witness statements. As he compared the case to others he's worked on, we heard the kind of stories that entertain on *The Sopranos* but sicken in real life. Bodies carted to Dumpsters. The rape and murder of a seven-year-old. Fifty stab wounds. Purdy reminisced about them as casually as if recalling a Yankees game.

He's seen stuff the rest of us never will. If ever someone has confronted the consequences that arise from a glaring absence of conscience, it's Bill Purdy.

"I've just finished listening to fifty hours of tapes about philosophy," he told me. "So to me conscience is an interesting philosophical concept. Whether it even exists or not. Is it innate? Learned? There's no hard evidence.

"If you ask me, Kennedy High School is a typical inner city school. I don't know the kids involved. I can just speculate. This is a difficult murder case. I've seen its kind before. With multiple defendants it will be hard to prove intent to kill. The jury charge will be to find defendants guilty only of that which they personally were responsible for. It may turn into aggravated manslaughter instead. That's ten to thirty years."

The phone rang constantly during our visit. "Prosecutor's office, Purdy," he would bark into the phone. "I'm not able to release that information." It wasn't clear whether he was speaking with reporters, family members, or defense attorneys. Each conversation was identical. Purdy plays by the rules and they don't often vary. When a call interrupted his train of thought, he circled back to the book I told him I was writing. "You want to write about conscience, huh?" he growled. "Most murders wouldn't happen if anyone gave them a second thought."

CONSCIENCE FLOWS LIKE A RIVER

ACTS OF CONSCIENCE flow through time like a river. They can pass by or around or under us unnoticed and then resurface at another time and place. There is permanence to them. They have a quality that nourishes and regenerates whatever they touch. There is no containing them. They breach walls, seep underground, and soar above barriers. This is the essence of their power.

No army is assured of such success. The most ruthless tyrant cannot command it. Acts of conscience are more powerful than both. Force aligned against them only infuses them with more energy and power, like water against a riverboat's wheel.

Like mighty rivers, acts of conscience reach all corners of the globe. They may disappear, as if they'd gone underground or simply evaporated, and then suddenly one day they rain down on us again. Five centuries later we are still captivated by St. Thomas More's fidelity to conscience over king, even at the expense of his life. Three hundred years after the Salem witch trials, Arthur Miller's *The Crucible* continues to light Broadway.

Acts of conscience can soothe like a fine mist, sting like slashing rain, or change the landscape with the unstoppable force of a tidal wave or raging torrent. They are used in ways that could never be foreseen. And they sustain life as surely as water and air.

Acts of conscience are timeless. How they will make themselves felt, and by whom, and under what circumstances, can never be predicted with certainty, only that they live on and take new forms.

An act taken in China may nurture a thousand others halfway around the world. How many times have you seen a poster of the brave student stopping a tank in Tiananmen Square? An individual's statement of fifty years ago may still resonate today. How many times have you heard a reference to Martin Luther King's "I Have a Dream" speech? The acts of ordinary private citizens like Rosa Parks and extraordinary public leaders like Gandhi create ripples that grow larger rather than smaller over time.

The ripples are obvious in how Thoreau and Tolstoy influenced Gandhi, who in turn influenced Dr. Martin Luther King, Jr. The Catholic Worker Dorothy Day influenced Thomas Merton, Daniel Berrigan, and successive generations of Catholic peace activists. On Good Friday 1969, farm labor organizer Cesar Chavez wrote a letter to E. L. Barr, Jr., president of the California Grape and Tree Fruit League, about his hopes for a strike and boycott. In that letter he quoted Dr. King.

And Dr. King himself, in his "Letter from a Birmingham jail," acknowledged:

Of course, there is nothing new about this kind of civil disobedience. It was evidenced sublimely in the refusal of Shadrach, Meshach and Abednego to obey the laws of Nebuchadnezzar, on the ground that a higher moral law was at stake. It was practiced superbly by the early Christians, who were willing to face hungry lions and the excruciating pain of chopping blocks rather than submit to certain unjust laws of the Roman Empire. To a degree, academic freedom is a reality today because Socrates practiced civil disobedience. In our own nation, the Boston Tea Party represented a massive act of civil disobedience.

ACTS OF CONSCIENCE CHANGE THE WORLD

PERHAPS NO ACT of conscience is better known or had greater impact than the refusal of a forty-two-year-old seamstress to give up her seat on the Cleveland Avenue bus to a white man in Montgomery, Alabama, on the first day of the last month of 1955.

Although Rosa Parks had been sitting in the row immediately behind the section of seats reserved for whites only, when another white man boarded the full bus, the driver ordered the blacks to relinquish the row and stand in the back. Three of the blacks did so, but Montgomery's racial customs required that all four blacks stand in order to allow one white man to sit, since no black was allowed to sit parallel to a white.

Parks shifted to the window side of the seat, but otherwise did not move. City law gave the driver the emergency police power to enforce the segregation codes, as well as the power to place Parks under arrest, which he did.

Local civil rights leaders saw two reasons for this to be the test case they'd been waiting for. First, even the segregation ordinances were not clear about a situation such as this, in which Parks had not sat in an area reserved for whites. And second, as Dr. Martin Luther King, Jr., explained to his congregation the next day, "Since it had to happen, I'm happy it happened to a person like Mrs. Parks for nobody can doubt the boundless outreach of her integrity. Nobody can doubt the height of her character, nobody can doubt the depth of her Christian commitment."

Rosa Parks's action touched off a 381-day boycott of the city's bus system, led by Dr. King, which is widely acknowledged as the beginning of the American civil rights movement. As Eldridge Cleaver, author of *Soul on Ice,* noted: "Somewhere in the universe, a gear in the machinery shifted."

To this day, world leaders remain influenced and inspired by her actions. Václav Havel, former president of the Czech Republic, describes Parks as a "sustainable hero" because "when her time came, she sat down."

And in the spring of 1989, when a lone Chinese student stood defiantly before an army tank in Beijing's Tiananmen

Square, South African president Nelson Mandela called it "a Rosa Parks moment."

The Rosa Parks story has been told many times, but her impact over generations is still revealing itself in new ways. In the first and only biography written about her, titled *Rosa Parks,* historian Douglas Brinkley tells of the mutual admiration between Parks and Mandela, who was five years her junior:

> Just four months after his release after spending twenty-seven years in the Robben Island prison for sabotage, Mandela had set out on a mission to make sure the United States would not lift its economic sanctions against still segregated South Africa. . . . After meeting with President George Bush and addressing the U.S. Congress in Washington, Mandela headed to Michigan. . . . "He's . . . always wanted to see Rosa Parks," explained Jesse Jackson, "and she is here."
>
> It was arranged for Parks to stand at the front of the receiving line, despite her protesting, "It's not proper. They don't need me. . . . He won't know me," Parks kept repeating, embarrassed that she had come.
>
> Moments later the airplane's door opened and Nelson Mandela . . . made his way down the steps and toward the receiving line. Suddenly he froze, staring open-mouthed in wonder. Tears filled his eyes as he walked up to the small old woman with her hair in two silver braids crossed atop her head. And in a low, melodious tone, Nelson Mandela began to chant, "Ro-sa Parks. Ro-sa Parks. Ro-sa Parks," until his voice crescendoed into a rapturous shout: "Ro-sa Parks!"

Then the two brave old souls, their lives so distant yet their dreams so close, fell into each other's arms, rocking back and forth in a long, joyful embrace. And in that poignant, redemptive moment, the enduring dignity of the undaunted afforded mankind rare proof of its own progress.

On July 3, 2002, *The New York Times* editorialized that Illinois governor George Ryan's declaration of a moratorium on the death penalty in Illinois "single-handedly instigated a new national debate on capital punishment by acting on conscience when faced with statistical evidence that innocent people stand a very real chance of being executed."

Since 1977, thirteen inmates on Illinois's death row had been exonerated, while twelve had been executed. Ryan himself had long been a supporter of the death penalty. But a *Chicago Tribune* investigation found that of two hundred sixty death penalty cases that had been appealed, at least half had been reversed.

Two and a half years later, on January 11, 2003, just forty-eight hours before the end of his term, Ryan commuted all Illinois death sentences to prison terms of life or less. He quoted Desmond Tutu, Abraham Lincoln, and Mahatma Gandhi.

Capital punishment weighs on those at both ends of the process. As Jim Willet, a former warden in Texas who presided over seventy-five executions, explained: "I'll be retiring next year and to tell you the truth, this is something

I won't miss a bit. You know, there are times when I'm standing there, watching those fluids start to flow, and wonder whether what we're doing here is right. It's something I'll think about for the rest of my life."

The *Times* editorial concluded: "By being the first governor to impose a moratorium on executions, Mr. Ryan has made it politically acceptable for conservative Republicans and Democrats alike to rethink capital punishment and how it is carried out. . . . The high standard calls into question the record of other death penalty states."

By March 2003, a judicial commission in Pennsylvania had recommended a moratorium for that state's death penalty.

A tenet of Jewish teaching is that when you save a life you save the entire world because you also save the lives of all of the children that life would have produced, and all of their children, and so on. Every one of us has the ability to do that. Every one of us has a strength to share and a conscience telling us to do so. Who among us has never had a chance to put a comforting hand on the shoulder of someone who was down or who others looked down upon?

The Christian theologian Dietrich Bonhoeffer wrote: "Conscience comes from a depth which lies beyond a man's own will and his own reason and it makes itself heard as the call of human existence to unity with itself. Conscience comes as an indictment of the loss of this unity and as a warning against the loss of one's self. It protests against a doing which imperils the unity of this being with itself. So long as conscience can be formally defined in these terms it is extremely inadvisable to act against its authority. . . . Action against one's own conscience runs parallel with suicidal action against one's own life, and it is not by chance that the two often go together."

SELECTIVE ASSERTIONS OF CONSCIENCE

> *It doesn't make sense that they're doing the show, with all these casualties. The juxtaposition of Hollywood going ahead with the Academy Awards while our soldiers and women and children are dying in Iraq is very mystifying—it's just stunning.*
>
> —*The New York Times,*
> March 24, 2003

> *The glorious, ridiculous, over-the-top orgy of gown and jewels and fantasies of conspicuous consumption—everything the red carpet entrance represents, was muted because of the war. . . . Tim Collins was there, waving a peace sign. . . . "I can't believe this silly show is going as bombs are falling." The 42-year-old musician thought it appalling and strange.*
>
> —*The Washington Post,*
> March 24, 2003

ON THE LAST day of 2002, *The New York Times* reported on the Israeli supreme court's ruling that reserve soldiers do not have a right to refuse to serve in the occupied territories of the West Bank and Gaza Strip. In explaining why selective assertions of conscience could not be permitted for the soldiers who had applied for conscientious objector status, the court found a distinction between refusing any service and refusing specific duties. The court explained, "The phenomenon of selective conscientious objection . . . raises in all its intensity the sensation of discrimination between 'one blood to another.'"

If it had looked for them, the Israeli supreme court could have found various selective assertions of conscience in America, especially during the war with Iraq, but also before and after.

The high point may have come with the countdown to the 2003 Academy Awards ceremony, which was dominated by Hollywood's self-created controversy about whether to hold it at all. A seemingly endless recitation of qualms about celebrating amid the fighting and dying in Iraq finally culminated in a decision to cancel only the red-carpet fashion extravaganza that traditionally precedes the ceremony itself.

Was this really the first time that pain and suffering around the globe coincided with the high-profile awards ceremony, or was it just the first time that the industry's nothing-if-not-trendy participants had been made aware of it?

When did the plight of humanity halfway around the world ever before interfere to this degree? The Academy Awards ceremony, like so many other rituals of our free and prosperous society, has long existed in juxtaposition to the misfortune and tragic suffering of those who dwell far outside our field of vision. Many places in the world that lack the security, liberty, and economic growth that we enjoy are instead haunted by violence, disease, and ruthless oppression. What made the death and destruction during the war in Iraq different for so many in Hollywood was that Americans were at risk, and as a result, the visibility of the issue in America was extraordinarily high.

In contrast to the round-the-clock cable coverage by "embedded" reporters transmitting live battle scenes, we don't have reporters with videophones embedded in the villages of the Congo, or the AIDS hospitals of South Africa, or the mountain hamlets of Indian Kashmir, or the famine-struck deserts of Ethiopia.

But just because we are not spoon-fed such suffering by the media does not mean it doesn't occur. In the same ten days of March 2003 that the Iraq war was taking place, so were the following:

The health ministry of Kenya reported that three people in Kenya die from AIDS every five minutes and about seven hundred die of HIV/AIDS-related complications daily.

At least five illegal immigrants were killed when fire swept through the Texas sugarcane field where they had fallen asleep while hiding.

One hundred fifty Congolese drowned when an overloaded ferry carrying two hundred passengers capsized in poor weather on Lake Tanganyika.

The death toll from a gas explosion in the Mengnanzhuang coal mine in Shanxi Province in northern China rose to thirty-five.

More than ten thousand people were left homeless after flooding swept away homes, roads, and maize crops in the hunger-stricken Gwembe district of Zambia.

All of these catastrophic developments could be found in major media like *The New York Times* and *The Washington Post*. But only if you searched hard and wore bifocals. The reporting was limited to a few small-print column inches of wire service dispatches in roundups of national or international news. They were not accompanied by photographs, interviews, special newspaper sections, or prime-time network television specials. There were no editorials or op-eds calling people to action. There were no campus debates or retired experts explaining why and how and what if.

There are legitimate reasons for Americans to devote their attention to the dangers, casualties, and deaths that befall their fellow countrymen. But what of the discrimination between "one blood to another" warned of by the Israeli supreme court? Are we so parochial that we prefer to ignore the agonies visited upon our fellow human beings when they lack the drama of war's televised images? Are we so shallow as not to realize that there is a human interest story behind every human loss? Are we so self-absorbed as to reserve our emotions and sympathies only for those who share our language and skin color? Are we so ignorant of recent history that we can't recognize that the world's troubles need not begin in our own backyard to land eventually right on our doorstep?

Selective assertion of conscience undermines the very calling of conscience itself. It casts shadows across conscience's guiding light. Conscience wasn't meant to be convenient, just rewarding. Conscience wasn't meant to make life easier, just fuller. With conscience we don't get to pick and choose, but rather choose and stick with the course we've picked.

Conscientious objection has a long and distinguished history here in the United States. While sixteen million Americans served in the military during World War II, forty-two thousand conscientious objectors refused to take arms. Judith Ehrlich, the producer of a documentary called *The Good War and Those Who Refused to Fight It,* explained, "The film is about the bravery required to have lived a life based on conscience. . . . It is harder to tell the story of these quiet heroes than the guys with the guns."

The Hollywood crowd that agonized over whether to go forward with Oscar night is the same crowd that has traditionally opted to tell the story of the guys with the guns. The truth, however, is not always as simple to communicate because it is not always as simple to know. Maybe that's why Senator John McCain has observed that "if Washington is a Hollywood for ugly people, Hollywood is a Washington for the simple-minded."

The plethora of needs faced by the world's huddled

masses is anything but simple. We couldn't meet them all even if we tried. But men and women of conscience have an obligation at least to learn for themselves rather than just listen to their leaders, to seek out facts and opinions beyond the narrow range conveyed between Fox News and CNN, to avoid selective assertions of conscience and instead search for truths.

V

The Conscience of Moral Entrepreneurs

Every man has a conscience, and finds himself observed by an inward judge which threatens and keeps him in awe . . . and this power which watches over the laws within him is not something which he himself (arbitrarily) makes, but it is incorporated in his being. . . .

—IMMANUEL KANT,
The Metaphysical Elements of Ethics

AN ENTREPRENEUR'S AMBITION

ON A SPRING morning in 1993 a well-dressed and very soft-spoken man walked into my office at Share Our Strength for a ten o'clock meeting. I had not met or heard of him before a mutual friend arranged our visit. He introduced himself and for the next two hours described what he called his "plans for the region." The intention was admirable and astonishingly ambitious—to create a new economy in Washington, along with the jobs, prosperity, and growth that went with it, and to do so in a way that benefited those most often left behind, the children of poor families without access to schools or quality health care.

He did not plan to do this on his own. Instead, he expected many of the wealthiest business leaders in Washington, Virginia, and Maryland to follow his lead. And soon they did. More than anyone ever dreamed.

Until then Washington, D.C., had long been a company town, and that company was the federal government. There were no other industries to speak of. The community was made up of hundreds of thousands of federal employees and the lawyers, lobbyists, and reporters who trolled for business in their wake. The region's economy had the virtue of being stable, if not dynamic. A new economy would be more than new, it would be a first.

The ambition of my visitor seemed audacious for a private citizen with none of the traditional power bases that matter so much to official Washington. He did not hold public office or know anyone who did. He had no track record in the community. He did not host the kind of Georgetown dinner parties where senators and *Washington Post* editors conspire to shape the national agenda. He wasn't even invited to them. Trying to create change in Washington without such status is like trying to farm without owning land. But like many individuals who'd benefited from the prosperity of the 1990s, he was exploring how best to give something back.

And there was a quality about Mario Morino that suggested he should not be underestimated, a combination of technical knowledge and street savvy, like a champion boxer who prevails not only because he has trained rigorously and perfected his punch, but because he understands more about the way his opponents think than they do.

Mario came from a career in technology and was enamored of its potential to do good. He was born in Pennsylvania coal country to a father who sold vacuum cleaners door to door and a mom who cleaned offices and houses. He held three union cards before enlisting in the U.S. Navy. Following a series of successful positions at General Motors, Eaton Manufacturing, and the Bureau of Naval Personnel, he created a set of systems management software products for mainframe computers and began a software company with an investment of six hundred dollars. He took the company public in 1986 and then merged to create Legent Corporation in 1989. Six years later it was a $500 million company with 2,800 employees. When it was sold to Computer Associates for $1.7 billion, it was the largest software acquisition in history at that time, managed by General Atlantic Partners in New York, one of the most successful groups of strategic investors in the world. Morino became a millionaire many times over.

Morino saw the benefits that technology would afford, saw them coming before anyone else, just as Barry Bonds could see the fastballs down the middle that would prove to be perfect home run pitches. His message that the Internet would change everything seems so obvious now as to obscure the fact that someone had to be the one to say it first. In this region, that someone was Mario. Technology was what he knew and what caused people to both respect and underestimate him at the same time. They respected his expertise and vision. They didn't realize that he understood people even better than he did computers.

I was somewhat self-conscious about having this wealthy stranger sitting on the other side of the chipped and battered folding table that I've used as a desk since founding Share Our Strength in 1984. In the nonprofit world it usually worked the other way around. Men like Mario did not come to us. Rather, my colleagues and I would find any excuse, travel any distance, cash in any chit, to obtain an audience with men like him. For philanthropic leaders and potential large donors to travel instead to our scrappy, makeshift office with its purple carpet and unframed posters tacked and taped askew to the walls, for them to sit there on folding chairs with their hands folded in their laps—well, it was almost unheard of.

There were plenty of times in his life he'd been told he couldn't do something, or more likely politely indulged by those who listened, nodded, and assumed they'd never hear from or of him again. Nothing fueled the motivation or competitive nature of this entrepreneur more.

ENTREPRENEURSHIP'S NEXT WAVE

THE ENTREPRENEUR ENJOYS cult status in the United States today. At the end of the last century, technological and business entrepreneurs transformed the American economy, forging information into an industry and creating more wealth more quickly than at any other time in history. Bill Gates at Microsoft, Jeff Bezos at Amazon, Pierre Omidyar with eBay, Steve Case for AOL, and countless others inspired a generation to innovate, take risks, and reap the rewards that come with designing the future.

Entrepreneurs have been defined many different ways. I think of them as jaywalkers, too impatient and resourceful to wait for the light to change. A nation that idolized and idealized the early pioneers who settled it found a new generation of them in its technology entrepreneurs. They embodied all of the great American myths: independence, the lone ranger taking on the system, guts and daring and defying the odds. They literally remade our world.

Following in their wake, and unabashed in their adoption and adaptation of entrepreneurial strategies and techniques, came social entrepreneurs, who are today changing the way civic and nonprofit organizations are run and managed. Social entrepreneurs introduce market forces into the nonprofit sector, like Bill Drayton at Ashoka, or like the Nature Conservancy. They measure social return on investment. From India to Indiana, from health care to housing, their innovations are ensuring that essential human needs are being met in ways that are more affordable, sustainable, and scalable than ever before.

After working closely with Mario Morino for nearly ten years—as friend, partner, and sometime consultant—I knew he was a different kind of entrepreneur, but I didn't know what kind until Jon Karp, my very patient editor at Random House, e-mailed me about a *New Yorker* magazine profile of Seventh Circuit Court of Appeals judge Richard Posner, a prolific writer who also teaches at the University of Chicago Law School. Politically conservative, grounded in free markets, Posner presents his opinions in an intellectually brash manner, which has earned him a reputation as a judicial provocateur. *The New Yorker* writes:

> What Posner really despises, though, is, as he sees it, the whining, sanctimonious pedantry of moral philosophers. . . . Posner contrasts the academic philosopher with what he calls "moral entrepreneurs" such as Martin Luther King or the feminist Catharine MacKinnon (whom Posner admires despite disagreeing with her politics): those who through sheer charisma and rhetorical force sweep people headlong out of their accustomed inertia and inspire new moralities altogether.

Moral entrepreneur is one of those perfect phrases that, in putting two large ideas next to each other, unexpectedly resolves false choices and illuminates new possibilities. *Moral entrepreneur* seems like an oxymoron. *Moral* implies a fixed compass point, something unyielding, stubbornly faithful and true to a conviction about right and wrong. An *entrepreneur,* on the other hand, though not amoral, is free from the orthodoxies of how things have always been done. He tries one thing and then another, discarding what doesn't work until he finds what does. Focus is on ends rather than means. Pragmatism rules. Entrepreneurs are jaywalkers, while morality rarely permits cutting corners. But forging together two often disparate concerns, moral entrepreneurs do what it takes to bring morality to places where it hasn't been before.

The idea of moral entrepreneurs who "inspire new moralities altogether" connotes something entirely different from social entrepreneurs. There are at least four principal distinctions.

Social entrepreneurs embrace business strategies to support sustainability and enhance the efficiency and effectiveness of social programs. *Moral entrepreneurs* embrace new responsibilities, making them their own, and persuade their peers to do likewise.

Social entrepreneurs build programs that work and expand them to scale. *Moral entrepreneurs* expand conscience, the fundamental prerequisite for concern, commitment, and action.

Social entrepreneurs build and lead new organizations. *Moral entrepreneurs* build and lead new movements. The mission of the *moral entrepreneur* is not to create a new tax-exempt organization. It is to inspire others to engage deeply in community causes and to do so in a way that leverages their unique strengths.

The passion of the *social entrepreneur* is to invent ways to do more with less, putting resources together in a way that represents more than the sum of their parts. The passion of the *moral entrepreneur* is to generate more so that more can be accomplished.

The *social entrepreneur* aims to remake the nonprofit sector, envisioning nonprofits behaving in different ways. The *moral entrepreneur* aims to remake the for-profit sector, envisioning people in for-profits behaving in different ways. By introducing a new ethic or a new way of being into an entire industry, they significantly leverage and widen their potential social impact.

Unlike social entrepreneurs, who introduce market forces into the nonprofit sector, moral entrepreneurs introduce moral principles into the for-profit sector. They change the way their colleagues in business think about their jobs and themselves by showing them why they need to get involved in their community and how to do so, and by helping them envision the impact they can have. They all but make it unfashionable not to. Coming from the private sector, they create vehicles designed to appeal to the interest of their peers in getting engaged.

Moral entrepreneurs intentionally influence society's leadership strata across all walks of life. By example and design they are redefining not only what it means to give back to society, but also what it will take to solve society's most pressing problems, whether in education, poverty, health care, child development, or other critical areas of need. Pioneering strategies of personal engagement and leverage, the moral entrepreneurs have the potential to unleash and mobilize the talents and resources of society's most successful individuals to address our most pressing needs. The product at the core of their business, far more complex than any software program, networked communications system, or even redesigned social service program, is the transformed conscience of their fellow human beings.

At the forefront of the field are remarkable individuals who embody its character and philosophy, innately talented and wildly successful in their own right, instructing others and inspiring us all. In most cases their rise was as unlikely as it was inevitable. But their own experience in surmounting obstacles convinced them that all such obstacles can be surmounted in this way. Their distinctive and expansive visions, personal persuasiveness, and indomitable will define what it means to be a moral entrepreneur today.

Moral entrepreneurs face far steeper challenges than do entrepreneurs in the for-profit sector. A moral entrepreneur succeeds only by getting others to grow, transform, and succeed. This is what makes the moral entrepreneur's impact so leveraged and significant. The moral entrepreneur's role is therefore decidedly a public one, not just private. It demands communication skills and powers of persuasion.

A DIFFERENT KIND OF ENTREPRENEUR

MARIO MORINO SAID he had come to the Share Our Strength offices to listen and learn. Unlike many who say that but then continue to do all the talking, he meant it. His passions were youth, learning, and community—three words he'd written on a legal pad just after retiring with his fortune—and over the next year he would meet with more than seven hundred people—educators, political leaders, clergy, business executives—in search of ideas that work. The combination of his perseverance, wealth, lack of personal agenda, and visionary track record won him an audience with key activists and opinion leaders whom he sought out methodically and relentlessly.

Forty-eight years old at the time we first met, Morino had the weary eyes and lined brow of someone who had worked hard for everything he'd attained. His net worth was north of $150 million and he could have just about anything he wanted. But his wants were so modest, so basic, that he'd used very little of it to accumulate any material goods. A nice house in the Virginia suburbs, but none of the other toys—no fast cars or boats, no long weekends in Europe, no equity stake in sports teams or movie companies, no climate-controlled wine cellar when a beer from the fridge would do just fine, thanks.

The weary eyes also exuded the confidence of someone whose best days were still ahead. And they would stay weary; though never taking a day's pay, he would work as hard at creating both a new economy and a new philanthropy as some of us work at just paying off our mortgage. From six in the morning until midnight, he worked every day, including most weekends.

As is the case with any such Cinderella story, a mythology grew up around Mario's personal style: his competitive nature, his long hours, and above all his prolific e-mails that often were waiting when you turned on your computer first thing in the morning, sent sometime between midnight and dawn, lurking behind your dark screen to pounce once you logged on.

His own energy radiated outward and pulled other people's energy toward him like a magnet. The physical properties of a room could be changed by his presence. With Mario at one end of a table, no matter where a meeting began or who ran it, it ended swirling around him, like water in a pan that once tilted has no chance of flowing anywhere else. There was a "Wizard of Oz" mystique to him, not only because he could make dreams come true, but also because many more people communicated with him than actually ever saw him. The Internet whose virtues he evangelized was also the curtain from behind which he operated.

Morino's personal demeanor was as modest as his ambitions were grandiose—a textbook example of what *Good to Great* author Jim Collins defined as Level V leadership—personally humble but professionally competitive. And in time Mario would achieve those ambitions. All but unheard of and unknown in Washington that spring morning in 1993, in just a few short years he would be a ubiquitous Washington figure, covered by *The Washington Post* and courted by national and regional politicians, a frequent keynoter at conferences on the Internet and philanthropy, and a widely sought board member for everything from the Brookings Institution to the Community Foundation. Indeed, it got to the point in the greater Washington area where it seemed as though all roads led through Mario. Academics, start-ups, venture capitalists, and politicians met him and met each other through him and found that there was only one degree of separation from him and then from each other.

Mario Morino's vision was not just about solving a problem, but about doing so by enlisting an army of activists who had never thought of themselves as any such thing. In this case, an army of wealthy colleagues who had also prospered from the region's remarkable boom, a boom Mario had a hand in creating. "Many of us should pinch ourselves to be sure we're not living in a wonderful fairy tale," he said again and again to anyone who would listen.

At the Deutsche Banc Alex. Brown Conference on June 27, 2000, Morino told the assembled: "Each of you—as entrepreneur, investor or investment banker—will experience a different sense of your responsibility beyond your business as your success grows. And whether it's your family roots, your faith, a cause near your family's heart, your desire to give back to your community, or even guilt with your success, you will make gifts to charity and take philanthropic actions in the years ahead. Ironically, few of you will apply the same rigor and discipline that made you successful in your business life to these actions. There are alternatives. . . ."

The alternative Morino had in mind was a fund he created in 2000 to invest in social programs that work, to build their capacity in a way that would enable them to reach scale. As he told the conference: "We define 'venture philanthropy' as the process of adapting strategic investment management practices to the nonprofit sector. . . . Under this model . . . investors would make a substantial long-term commitment focused exclusively on building capacity. . . . In addition to gifts of equity—the investment—these givers would also share their managerial and technological expertise. They would leverage their network of contacts."

After more than a year of laying the groundwork, Morino raised more than $30 million for his fund in a matter of weeks from others who'd prospered from the economic boom driven by the technology sector and were looking for a strategic way to give back. Who they were was as significant as how much they gave. They included AOL founder Steve Case and his wife, Jean; Virginia's governor-elect, Mark Warner; Raul Fernandez of Proxicom; Jack Davies (former president of AOL International); and many others.

By 1998, when First Lady Hillary Clinton came to keynote the Washington Philanthropy Summit, a breakfast that attracted almost eight hundred business leaders, they would find it sponsored by Fannie Mae, the *Washington Business Journal,* and a small family-named foundation called the Morino Institute.

Mario's investors did not get just a receipt for their money. They got briefing books and PowerPoint presentations, and investor dinners where they not only met the Venture Philanthropy Partners staff and the investment partners, but also got to socialize with the other investors themselves. Mario envisions these investors using more than money to make charitable organizations more effective. As he told *Regardie's* magazine, "Today, most of the money that's given to charities is programmatic. We reward the nonprofits that have lowest overhead. Therefore, we're telling them, 'don't manage, don't plan, don't build future capacity, don't market your services to people who could benefit from them.' That's the opposite of what you do in building a business."

Morino became a mentor to other entrepreneurs, helping them find support, make contacts, and share ideas. As one entrepreneur once said: "Mario is the kind of guy who does the right thing even if no one is looking."

IN THE KITCHEN

MORAL ENTREPRENEURS HAVE always been at the heart of the dynamic growth of Share Our Strength, the national antihunger and antipoverty organization I founded almost two decades ago. They are the reason we've raised more than $150 million. They range from the world's most acclaimed chefs with their own boutique restaurants to CEOs of some of the world's largest restaurant chains and food processing companies, from the authors of best-selling novels to the founders of global lifestyle footwear and apparel brands.

Moral entrepreneurship is what Danny Meyer has demonstrated by leveraging his ownership of just a few restaurants to influence a broad swath of the New York and national restaurant industry to engage in a wide range of philanthropic activities from hunger relief to community development.

Like Mario Morino, Meyer's principal expertise is not in solving social problems. But the professional expertise of each is so widely regarded that others in their profession have been persuaded to follow their lead in undertaking to solve social problems.

Danny Meyer's early interests were political. After college he interned on Capitol Hill and volunteered on the presidential campaign of independent candidate John Anderson. Starting out in business, he purposely identified locations for each of his four restaurants in neighborhoods where success would also help build community. He opened Union Square Cafe in 1985, about the same time that Share Our Strength was beginning. It was a critical success from the outset, garnering the coveted three-star *New York Times* rating. When Gramercy Tavern opened in 1994, Danny became the first restaurateur ever to place two restaurants in the Zagat "Top 10." Now this small-businessman has six hundred employees, and customers from Wall Street, law, publishing, and the national press corps. And because he is one of the most successful restaurateurs not only in New York but also across the nation, he has sent the message that social activism can be good for business.

When you walk into one of Danny Meyer's restaurants,

you start feeling good even before the meal begins. The purpose of the restaurant is not just to feed you. It is to give you the experience of being cared for. Danny calls such caring "enlightened hospitality," which he defines as "caring for each other; caring for our guests; caring for our community; caring for our suppliers; and finally, caring for profitability."

Like all great innovations, Danny's vision of pairing great food with caring service and easy comfort seems obvious now, but that's because it has been so widely imitated. "The single most important thing to me in putting together a new restaurant is choosing a great staff. When we hire, what we look for first are emotional skills. We require intelligence, of course, but techniques can be taught. Someone can be trained to put the knife and fork in a certain place. But caring for people almost has to be intuitive."

Danny's genius was to find ways to take "caring for people" to scale. The same philosophy that made his restaurants successful imbued his commitment to community. Caring was not something to be confined to his own customers and employees. He needed it to extend beyond the doors of his own establishments.

Inspired by his personal example and persuaded by his personal pleas, hundreds of chefs and restaurateurs today find themselves cooking at food and wine benefits, teaching nutrition and food budgeting skills to low-income families, and advocating for policies that promote sustainable agriculture. They participate in Taste of the Nation, buy produce from the Union Square green market, donate surplus food to City Harvest, and participate in many other food and wine benefits for causes ranging from juvenile diabetes to domestic violence.

Danny Meyer was not the first chef or restaurateur to become involved in this way, and he is not alone. But along with a small handful of colleagues like Alice Waters, Pano Karatassos, and others of like mind, he has made such service to community a rite of passage. Many young chefs are introduced to it as early as culinary school. It is so pervasive that it might as well be part of the written job description.

IN COCKPITS AND MUD HUTS

I'D NEVER BEFORE flown with a pilot whose pre-flight checklist included conducting a group prayer, but that's what ours did before we took off in a six-seat single-engine Cessna across the vast desert to drought-devastated Gode in southern Ethiopia. If there was a dangerous part of our weeklong assessment of the non-governmental organizations (NGOs) working to avert mass famine in Ethiopia, this was it.

Our pilot, Captain Herman van Heuvelen, is the director of flight operations for the Mission Aviation Fellowship (MAF), a faith-based organization of four hundred pilots who fly humanitarian missions into places no one else will go. It was established by a World War II pilot named Jim Truxton and two other pilots in 1943. Its fleet of sixty-eight aircraft enables pilots to transport missionaries and humanitarian relief supplies across rough and hostile terrain that could otherwise take days or weeks by camel, foot, or boat. All of the planes are donated, and Captain van Heuvelen supports himself and his wife and five children by writing newsletters to friends and family soliciting their support. The pilots fly many different aircraft, from single-engine Cessnas to pressurized twin-engine King Air 200s, operating in jungles and deserts and from mountain landing strips.

Because all six seats of the plane were filled, van Heuvelen asked me to take the co-pilot seat and to put on the headphones so we could talk. He told me that he flew F-16s for Holland's Royal Air Force before training at the MAF's bush pilot school in Redlands, California.

He came to Ethiopia after spending eight straight years flying relief supplies into, and medevacs out of, Uganda. "Often we need to use runways that were abandoned seven or eight years ago. That's why we only use these single-engine planes. They need next to no runway. Can get in and out of anywhere. A twin-engine needs a longer runway because it needs to gain much greater speed to compensate for weight and balance. A single-engine can land and take off anywhere. The only problem," he said with a shrug, "is if you lose the engine."

From an altitude of only 9,500 feet, the view of the desert was staggering. It hadn't rained for three and a half years in this region, and it was immediately clear why relief officials found it almost impossible to get adequate food, water, and medical supplies to the nomadic pastoralists, who had lost more than 90 percent of their herds. There are no paved roads, and even by plane, Gode is two and a half hours away. When it finally did rain, just about two weeks before we arrived, bridges washed away and the dirt roads became impassable.

Before I got to Africa, I didn't really understand why the drought's impact was so devastating. But in the southern region of Ethiopia, the pastoralists live dramatically different lives. They don't buy their food at the store or market, they don't farm and raise a diverse range of crops, they certainly don't have charitable organizations to serve them. Instead, these eight million Ethiopians do what their nomadic ancestors have done for thousands of years, relentlessly herding goats, sheep, cattle, and oxen in search of water, living off the milk and meat, criss-crossing a continent again and again for the sole purpose of survival. Life in Ethiopia and the quest for water in Ethiopia are one and the same. It is not a seasonal quest, but a daily one. Women walk ten hours a day to bring home their families' water needs. Not just on market days, or rainy days, but every day, day after day, week after week, for months, years, decades.

From Jim Truxton in 1943 to Captain van Heuvelen today, the pilots of the MAF represent the unique kind of entrepreneurs that could be called moral entrepreneurs. They've literally transformed weapons of war, built to unleash awesome destructive firepower, into daring tools of peace. Trained and skilled in the art of combat, they introduced a new morality into their elite fraternity of aviators—the art of delivering humanitarian aid and peace. Thanks to the Mission Aviation Fellowship, air force pilots the world over have an alternative avenue today for sharing their strength.

When we left Gode, Captain van Heuvelen explained, "They can't even clear me for takeoff at this airport." He pointed to a rickety wood tower. "No one has been in that tower for years. There's someone inside a building somewhere, but since they have no visual, all they can do is wish me good luck."

When I flew to Ethiopia in May 2000, at the onset of a drought that killed the herds of cattle and goats the desert nomads depend upon for meat and milk, the people were hungry and sick. Children were being carried for hours across the desert to clinics, and some perished from starvation and dehydration.

Our host, teacher, and leader was Abera Tola, a soft-spoken thirty-nine-year-old who lives in a quiet neighborhood high on a hill overlooking Addis Ababa. Abera speaks softly, as befits wise words that deserve to be leaned into. He is a reluctant leader, born with attributes and tempered by circumstances that made assuming some responsibility for his people almost inevitable. His father was a large landowner. His degrees are advanced and from abroad. He is slated for the leadership of his tribe.

Abera had charted our journey and showed us the hardest-hit regions to which we would travel. The map of Ethiopia doesn't lie, but it can deceive. It certainly can't convey the enormity of the ancient Rift Valley, a vast landscape with no horizon, dotted with round thatched-roof houses that are so small on the dry land they look like caramel candies that spilled in your yard.

On the map, the road to Yabello is a thick, brightly colored orange stripe that looks as if it could be the Pennsylvania Turnpike. There is a route sign on the map, like our interstate shields, that says Route 6 as if it were a real road. How would you know that it is unpaved and jammed with sheep, goats, mules, and chickens? That villagers by the hundred stand chatting in the middle, not quite ignoring the rare Land-Rover that roars by, but just barely shifting their weight to avoid being hit by the vehicle with its horn bleating, passing not within inches but fractions of inches?

What's most exciting is not what the international agencies are doing, but what the Ethiopians are doing for themselves. A generation of their best and brightest have given more of themselves than anyone has a right to expect.

In 1994, Abera Tola created HUNDEE, a nonprofit whose mission is to promote civic education and development at the grassroots level by providing seed money for poor households to establish micro-enterprises. By 1999 he was taking courses at Harvard's Kennedy School of Government. Then Abera brought his learning back to Ethiopia. Today he leads the efforts of Share Our Strength partner Oxfam, coordinating strategy and resources for local development efforts.

In between appointments one afternoon toward the end of our visit, Abera said, "My story is kind of long and complicated." His father's land had been confiscated by the government, and in the 1980s, because of his political views, Abera was imprisoned for ten years by the Dergue, which created a police state after forcibly seizing power.

Two of those years were spent in what Abera described as an interrogation prison. "The interrogation room, it's like a small—no, a big garage. And all of the tools that were usually on a garage wall, they were there in the interrogation room, but to torture you, to humiliate you. They put things in your mouth, beat you with things, shocked you, spun you around." Abera explained that his cellmate was a chain smoker. "Cigarettes can be your friend. You can watch their smoke and follow it to other places where you'd like to go."

After two years in the interrogation prison, Abera was moved to the central prison, which housed six hundred prisoners in just twelve rooms. Abera was in a sixteen-square-meter room with fifty-three other men. They slept with their heads at one another's feet, holding them for warmth, as you would a teddy bear, and also to avoid getting a kick in the face.

This is the Abera I don't know and never will. Even if he talked about it more than rarely, which he does not, it falls beyond the pale of even my imagination. We have enjoyed hearty meals on two continents and met each other's families but I can never know this. Just as I can never truly understand the choices he's made, and whether he has regrets, and if so, how he lives with them. He is of Ethiopia but he is also apart from it, like a member of an elite club, characterized by the way he dresses and reads and e-mails friends on the other side of the globe. I wonder how he's overcome his bitterness. Perhaps the best one can do is contain it. Abera exhibits a certain carefulness, a polite wariness. He can go long periods without saying a word. He has learned to be self-contained.

Up one morning with the roosters in remote Yabello, before dawn's first light, I watched Abera walk with a water bucket to the foul dark latrine dug into the ground behind our $1.10 rooms. I thought of the simple pleasures he must have enjoyed sitting at a Starbucks near Harvard Square, and the way his eyes came alive when he talked about the rows of books he browsed in Cambridge's many bookstores. I wondered if he thinks of this or longs for the comfortable life that was his, that could yet be his, but for the quiet steady commitment to his homeland and the unfinished—perhaps unfinishable—business at hand.

MORAL ENTREPRENEURS IN ALL SHAPES AND SIZES

THIS IS THE power of moral entrepreneurs: They create a desire to give back to the community. The spread of such an ethic can't be legislated. Nor can it be decreed by executive order or judicial fiat. Danny Meyer and Mario Morino didn't have to run for office to promote the types of behavior that solve social problems. Instead, they searched to understand how to do the right thing, then communicated it, after proving that it didn't come at the expense of success but rather enhanced it. In each case their inspiration was conveyed from peer to peer, one person reaching another, then two influencing four, and four eight, until a geometric progression was achieved.

By introducing the business world to social activism, they have revolutionized the way resources are brought to bear on social issues. The results have been concrete and dramatic. More children are being fed, housed, educated. More parents are receiving the support they need to provide for their kids.

The examples of Danny Meyer and Mario Morino also help underscore another critical distinction. An ever-increasing number of socially responsive business leaders are purposeful about ensuring that their companies are good corporate citizens. This may manifest itself in their community relations, environmental practices, employment and human resources policies, and other areas of business management. While this trend is admirable and needed, this behavior makes them good corporate citizens but does not make them moral entrepreneurs. The latter term is reserved only for those who have introduced a moral dimension into new communities.

It would be a disservice to people like Danny and Mario not to make one caveat explicit: the fact that those who introduce moral principles into an economic community are labeled "moral entrepreneurs" is not meant to imply that they themselves are more moral than the rest of us. That would be an unfair burden to saddle on good people, almost certainly setting them up to fail. And it misses the point. Moral entrepreneurs focus on public moralities, not the private ones that are appropriately the province of individuals, their families, and their conscience.

There are a number of other instructive examples of moral entrepreneurs:

Jeff Swartz, president and CEO of Timberland, has worked to make justice part of the promise of the global lifestyle brand Timberland as it expands from boots and footwear to include apparel for men, women, and children. "Doing well and doing good are inextricably linked. Commerce and justice. They are organically part of the same action. Everything you do is for the benefit of the shareholder and the benefit of the employee in the context of the community and with respect to the consumer."

Achievements include the company's ongoing commitment to move boot-making processes away from hazardous materials, the company's policy of allocating forty paid hours a year for community service, and their partnership with City Year have set industry standards.

The company has also insisted that the factories around the world that employ the more than thirty thousand people involved in manufacturing Timberland products meet certain standards and fair labor practices that, while mandated by the laws of those countries, are traditionally ignored.

In 1971, Bernard Kouchner co-founded Médecins Sans Frontières, or Doctors Without Borders, the world's first non-governmental organization specializing in emergency medical assistance. It created a vehicle for physicians everywhere to think differently about the power they have to make a difference in the world. Today it is an organization with offices in eighteen countries and more than 2,500 medical doctors volunteering in more than eighty countries. Most important, they recognized that they could help shape public opinion through the enormous power of the media, which changed the nature of aid agency advocacy. They have worked in Thailand, Yugoslavia, El Salvador, Rwanda, Afghanistan, and Iraq.

It is common today for rock stars and musicians to use their talent to raise money and awareness for causes ranging from famine in Africa to farm policies in the United States. But this wasn't always the case. It took moral entrepreneurs to transform the music industry, and one of the first was former

Beatle George Harrison. In August 1971, George Harrison organized the Concert for Bangladesh, a two-day event in Madison Square Garden to raise money to aid that desperately poor country. The concert was arranged on short notice following a call from Harrison's friend Ravi Shankar, the Indian sitar player. The concert raised money exceeding all expectations.

The Concert for Bangladesh is widely considered to be the pivotal event in the evolution of musical activism. It would be followed by Bob Geldof's 1985 Live Aid concert, Amnesty International concerts, Willie Nelson's Farm Aid concerts, and others, as musicians realized that they had a role to play in mobilizing world opinion. As singer David Crosby explained in his documentary *Stand and Be Counted,* "Our main job is to be entertainers, but the other part is for us to be the town crier, the troubadour, to say 'It's twelve o'clock and all is well,' or 'It's twelve-thirty and it's not so good.'"

Among the many other performers who have embraced this role are Sting, Bono, Harry Belafonte, Eric Clapton, Bob Dylan, Tracy Chapman, and Joan Baez.

Oseola McCarty was a washerwoman from Hattiesburg, Mississippi, who saved the dollars she made taking in laundry and ironing to create a $150,000 scholarship fund so that complete strangers could get a college education at the University of Southern Mississippi in her hometown. "I'm giving it away so that the children won't have to work so hard like I did," she said on July 15, 1995, when she established the irrevocable trust, explaining that "there's a lot of talk about self-esteem these days. It seems pretty basic to me. If you want to feel proud of yourself, you've got to do things you can be proud of. Feelings follow actions."

McCarty herself never made it past the sixth grade. Born in 1908, she dropped out of Eureka Elementary School to take care of a sick aunt. She never married or owned a car, and she left Mississippi only once in her first eighty-seven years. Supporting herself by taking in washing and ironing, initially for $1.50 to $2 a bundle, she says that it was when "I started making $10 a bundle phat I commenced to save some money. I put it in savings. I never would take any of it out. I just put it in. It just accumulated."

The impact of her action was more far-reaching than she could have imagined. It was as if she'd called a bluff at a poker game and then sat back to watch other players toss their chips on the pile. Contributions from more than six hundred other donors added over $330,000 to the original scholarship fund. Ted Turner, the founder of CNN, was inspired to donate $1 billion to the United Nations health and population programs, saying, "If that little woman can give away everything she has, then I can give a billion."

Oseola McCarty died of liver cancer in September 1999 in the frame house where she took in laundry and ironing and made her fortune a dollar or two at a time. She lived long enough to see herself honored with the Presidential Medal of Freedom from President Clinton, an honorary doctorate from Harvard, and the privilege of carrying the Olympic torch. She must have known she wouldn't live to see the recipients of her scholarships graduate, but that's not why she was doing it. As she told a *New York Times* reporter, "I can't do everything, but I can do something to help somebody. And what I can do I will do."

Finally, in May 2001 I received a letter from Scott Wilkerson, a forty-five-year-old man in Tampa Bay, Florida, who explained:

> I owned a group of automobile dealerships (650 employees, $275 million in sales) for 18 years. I began with one small, financially struggling dealership in 1982 that became the nation's largest and most profitable Lincoln-Mercury store, as well as having the highest customer satisfaction rating throughout the Ford Motor Company. My philosophy was to focus on long-term profitability through customer satisfaction and to attain customer satisfaction through employee satisfaction. We added three more dealerships in the Bay Area in the late 1980s.
>
> Beginning in 1990 I focused my full attention on creating a more civil and respectful business model than the traditional paternalistic model used in the for-profit world. . . . My belief is that a business can become a place that honors the human spirit while accomplishing the necessary profit objec-

tives. I also believe the burden is on the leadership of an organization and that the managers must be willing to do their own inner work in order to become the compassionate servant leaders needed to make the workplace a safe and respectful environment.

Scott developed a business plan for a chain of car dealerships that an organization like Share Our Strength would own. Unlike many good ideas, this one came with someone who had the ability to achieve it. Scott is so passionate about helping kids that he committed to come out of retirement and personally run the business.

Scott is the classic American entrepreneur. But he is more than that. He is among the new breed of moral entrepreneurs who see the need and opportunity to introduce moral principles into the industries in which they work.

Changing the world depends on changing the people in it. The message common to each of these stories is not just that having been successful, each of these people felt an obligation to give back (though they surely believed that to be the case). That is not a new idea. It has been part of a tradition of *noblesse oblige* that runs from Andrew Carnegie through Bill Gates and beyond. Rather, these individuals promulgate and model an even more powerful idea: that the very skills and practices that made them successful in their life's first chosen arena of commerce must also be deployed on behalf of the social problems they wish to solve.

The net effect is to redefine what it means to be an entrepreneur, to recalibrate expectations and responsibilities. In New York a chef is no longer expected only to cook fine food. Serving the community by volunteering or helping to cook at benefits is also an integral part of the job.

Moral entrepreneurship has less to do with the inflexible dogmas of moral certainty than with introducing elements of morality into places one long took for granted as morally neutral. It contemplates a world in which a chef is more than a chef, a doctor more than a doctor, a world in which a central question that each of us asks and answers is how our professional skills can be deployed beyond our profession, not only in the service of profit, but so others can profit from our service.

Moral entrepreneurs work at points of great leverage. While their professions and social interests are diverse, they usually have these five things in common:

Consistent professional success has put them near the top of their field and earned the respect of their peers. They have enjoyed financial security, favorable press, and expanded contacts.

They are purposeful in capturing knowledge about the ingredients of that success, whether customer service, marketing, or quality assurance, and applying those ingredients in the social arena.

Their principal experience comes from outside the nonprofit sector, in business, entertainment, art, medicine.

They are more pragmatic than political, committed more to performance than to ideology.

They leverage their networks, beginning with those closest to them, and those networks are often rich in resources and skills.

The new methods ushered in by social entrepreneurs have been badly needed and are also certain to change with the times, as methodologies must. But the new moral dimension introduced by moral entrepreneurs is likely to bring sweeping and lasting change as they redefine entire professions and industries. There are still many industries left to find their way, perhaps waiting for a moral entrepreneur to lead them.

"Moral entrepreneur" is a new term, but moral entrepreneurs themselves are anything but new. They have existed throughout history and have been among the principal drivers of civilization's progress. Just as the innovation of one entrepreneur sets the stage for another's activity, as the invention of the microchip led to the development of the laptop, the same is true of moral entrepreneurs, as one act of conscience creates a climate of inspiration and support for the next.

Moral leaders like King and Gandhi are wonderful inspirational icons, but their utility as role models is more limited. They were unique individuals alive at unique times in the world's history. Most of us couldn't lead the kind of lives they led. But the footsteps of a Danny Meyer or a Mario Morino can be followed by many. Moral entrepreneurship is not reserved for a handful of history's greats who come along once a century or so, but is something we can all apply in our daily lives.

VI

The Conscience of Leaders

Labor to keep alive in your breast that little spark of celestial fire called conscience.

—GEORGE WASHINGTON

LEAD OR FOLLOW?

AT ANY AIRPORT newsstand you will find the book section dominated by books on leadership and other business best-sellers. The businesspeople who pass by in waves, en route to whatever next deal they are certain will give them a competitive edge, are seen as the ideal audience for advice on getting to the head of the pack. Considerable real estate at Borders and Barnes & Noble is devoted to the same popular topic.

One such popular paperback, a book with a gold stamp promoting its status as a "*Business Week* Bestseller," is called *Elizabeth I, CEO: Strategic Lessons from the Leader Who Built an Empire*. It was written by Alan Axelrod, a former college professor turned consultant who I'm willing to bet is a good man, smart, and well-intentioned. The premise of his book is that understanding how Elizabeth I ruled her empire can enable one better to lead one's business, whether it be a soft-serve ice cream shop or an Internet service provider.

Axelrod's book is in good company. Leadership books abound today, swamping the nonfiction best-seller lists and launching careers for consultants and motivational speakers. A few such books are published by serious scholars who have researched leaders throughout the ages and taught and refined history's tried and true lessons. Warren Bennis and Peter Drucker come to mind for the depth and breadth of their work. But the real consumer market is for a very different kind of book, the books about leadership written by and about anyone (dead or alive!) who has enjoyed success and has been in the public eye, which is the working definition of expertise in our society today. This makes leadership experts of generals, coaches, athletes, business leaders, even Arctic explorers. They include, to name just a few:

Lincoln on Leadership: Executive Strategies for Tough Times by Donald T. Phillips

Leadership Secrets of Colin Powell by Oren Harari

Leading with the Heart: Coach K's Successful Strategies for Basketball, Business and Life by Duke University's legendary basketball coach Mike Krzyzewski

Jesus CEO: Using Ancient Wisdom for Visionary Leadership by Laurie Beth Jones

Patton on Leadership: Strategic Lessons for Corporate Warfare by *Elizabeth I, CEO* author Alan Axelrod

Shackleton's Way: Leadership Lessons from the Great Antarctic Explorer by Margot Morrell et al.

It's Your Ship: Management Techniques from the Best Damn Ship in the Navy by D. Michael Abrashoff

Power Plays: Shakespeare's Lessons in Leadership and Management by John O. Whitney

This veritable library presents a delicious irony. The premise of most of the books is that the surest path to leadership is following someone else. The core theory implicit to all is that leadership is learned from studying others rather than through the sometimes painful task of getting to know one's true self. Their most earnest advice is not to think for oneself, nor to learn from one's own experiences, but to try to think the way some successful celebrity does or did.

The strong sales figures and widespread dissemination of such books would suggest that there must be many other Lincolns, Colin Powells, and Shackletons walking around in our midst, and that in turn there is great confidence today in those who lead our political, business, and religious institutions. Or does the scarcity of such greatness cast doubt upon the efficacy of these popular but clichéd volumes? Perhaps the one thing more disadvantageous, even dangerous, than the paucity of Lincolns, Powells, and Shackletons is the likelihood that considerably inferior mortals will think they possess such attributes after skimming a few hundred pages.

It wouldn't take much to test this thesis. Define for yourself who you consider to be a great leader, whether an international or national figure or simply someone with whom you work or play. Now search for even a shred of evidence that they got there by following advice from *Business Week* or a best-selling leadership book. Many of us fear that the great leaders are a vanishing breed. Maybe now we've hit on a correlation.

There is another genre of leadership books that readers might find even more perplexing. These include:

The 7 Habits of Highly Effective People by Stephen Covey
The Five Temptations of a CEO by Patrick Lencioni
The 21 Irrefutable Laws of Leadership by John Maxwell
The 17 Indisputable Laws of Teamwork by John Maxwell
10 Keys to Servant Leadership by Calvin Miller
The 17 Principles of Personal Achievement by Napoleon Hill
The 9 Natural Laws of Leadership by Warren Black
The Seven Laws of Christian Leadership
The Stuff of Heroes—The Eight Universal Laws of Leadership
Six Sigma
Beyond Success: The 15 Secrets to Effective Leadership and Life Based on Legendary Coach John Wooden's Pyramid of Success

With few exceptions, good advice seems to come only in odd-numbered sets. This is just a small sampling. But the math is intimidating. At best the experts contradict one another. At worst, if they are right, there are apparently hundreds of secrets, keys, principles, habits, and laws to be mastered by anyone who desires to lead. That's a lot for even the most committed student of leadership to remember. Plus there will always be the dilemma of deciding, in a given situation, whether to do what Queen Elizabeth I would have done or what Coach K would have done. They had pretty different styles.

Nor is there a shortage of such material in business magazines and journals. In the June 2002 issue of *Fast Company* magazine, an article in the "best practice" category is called "The Strategy of the Fighter Pilot." The premise of the article is that "business is a dogfight. Your job as a leader is to outmaneuver the competition, respond to fast-changing conditions and defeat your rivals." The learnings of legendary fighter pilot John Boyd are proposed as the key to doing that.

Of course, pointers and strategies based on experience are always helpful, but this entire leadership-advice industry is built upon what is hiding in plain sight: one's own sense of right and wrong, that is, one's conscience. One or two such books might have sneaked by harmlessly on their own, entertaining and informative. But when they are taken together, complete with copycats and cheap knockoffs, the full measure of ridicule deserved by this genre becomes especially obvious.

Bruce Pasternack, senior vice president of the consulting firm Booz Allen in San Francisco, writes, "The last time I checked, there were 393 current books with the words 'leader' or 'leadership' in their titles. . . . When one peeks between the covers of such texts, disappointment soon sets in. The sad fact is that leadership manuals deliver mainly truisms, pap, and gross generalizations."

This is not to suggest that leadership is an unimportant topic or that understanding and cultivating it are not worthy objectives. Leadership is probably the most important variable in organizational performance, whether business, military, athletic, or nonprofit. Leaders are indispensable to setting the tone, vision, and culture of an enterprise. But genuine leadership is a rare and distinguishing factor. Like anything else, the value we place on it tells us something about how uncommon it is. This is a dependable clue to the odds against relying on manuals to make leaders. The question of whether leaders are born or made is age-old and may never be answered definitively. But the question of whether leaders can be made from the kind of "pulp nonfiction" so popular among mid-level managers today can be answered with less ambivalence and greater economy: NO.

CONSCIENCE-DRIVEN LEADERSHIP

IN DECEMBER 2001, the *Harvard Business Review* (*HBR*) published the first "special issue" in its seventy-nine-year history.

The subject of the special issue was "breakthrough leadership." It included original articles and reprints by the best-selling leadership gurus: Tom Peters, John Kotter, Daniel Coleman, and Ronald Heifetz. They write about "Primal Leadership: The Hidden Driver of Great Performance," and "Leadership in a Combat Zone," and "The Work of Leadership."

These experts variously define leaders as those who "set the vision," "energize people," "choose the right people," "motivate," "communicate the values of the organization," "insist that people surpass themselves," or "force disputes to the surface." They make the case that leadership is about "coping with change," "a sense of the future," or "fielding the best team."

The *HBR* special issue on leadership is 148 pages long. The word "conscience" doesn't appear on one of them, nor does the concept of conscience-grounded leadership. I was not surprised. Not because I don't think business leaders have consciences. They do. But because espousing conscience-driven leadership would all but put the growing industry of leadership gurus out of business. Why? Because it is so simple. It's not the *word* I'm hung up on, but rather the *concept*. What could be easier or more natural than conscience-grounded and conscience-driven leadership? What could require less external coaching or instruction? A leadership based on the one thing you can be more sure of than any other variable: what your own conscience tells you is right.

Although the issue of whether leaders are born or can be made by reading the *Harvard Business Review* and other such publications remains an open question, the appetite for instruction on leadership is unquestionable and virtually insatiable. Leadership is seen as the key to unlocking performance, results, and those twin gods of success: fortune and fame. Stanford University's business school offers an executive education program, the largest block of which is on leadership and strategy and includes courses such as "Teams Without Boundaries," "Leading Change and Organizational Renewal," and "Managing Teams for Innovation and Success."

There are compelling examples of conscience-driven leadership and the business success to which it can lead.

Katharine Graham transformed *The Washington Post* from an average newspaper into a powerful and profitable brand, and as she made clear in her Pulitzer Prize–winning *Personal History,* it wasn't through an innate understanding of either journalism or the newspaper business and its economics. She felt entirely unprepared to assume control of the paper upon her husband's death. What she fell back on was her gut instincts of right and wrong. In fact she risked the company's reputation and its business on what she did know: that it was right to publish both the Pentagon Papers and the work of Woodward and Bernstein that broke the Watergate story:

During these months, the pressures on the *Post* to cease and desist were intense and uncomfortable. I was feeling beleaguered. Many of my friends were puzzled about our reporting. Joe Alsop was pressing me all the time. And I had a distressing chance meeting with Henry Kissinger just before the election. "What's the matter? Don't you think we're going to be reelected?" Henry asked me. Readers, too, were writing to me, accusing the *Post* of ulterior motives, bad journalism, lack of patriotism.

Nixon's campaign to undermine public confidence in the *Post* was intensifying. . . . Bearing the full brunt of presidential wrath is always disturbing. Sometimes I wondered if we could survive four more years of this kind of strain.

The timing of these challenges made them potentially devastating, coming not only in the thick of Watergate but also just a year and a half after the Pentagon Papers and after the company had gone public with its stock.

Among the worst effects was the sharp decline in our stock price that naturally ensued, from $38 a share down to $28 in the first two weeks after the challenges, and continuing on down to $16 or $17, decreasing the value of the company by more than half. . . .

I have often been credited with courage for backing our editors in Watergate. The truth is that I never felt there was much choice. There was never one major decisive moment when I, or anyone, could have suggested that we stop reporting the story. Watergate unfolded gradually. By the time the story had grown to the point where the size of it dawned on us, we had already waded deeply into its stream. Once I found myself in the deepest water in the middle of the current, there was no going back.

Mrs. Graham guided *The Washington Post* through two of the most celebrated episodes in American journalism, the publication in 1971 of the Pentagon Papers, a secret government history of the war in Vietnam, and the Watergate scandal, which led to Richard M. Nixon's resignation from the presidency in 1974 under the threat of impeachment. She and Benjamin C. Bradlee, the editor she chose to run the *Post*'s newsroom during her years at the helm, transformed the *Post* and its reputation.

"She set the newspaper on a course that took it to the very top ranks of American journalism in principle and excellence and fairness," said Bradlee, now a *Post* vice president. "That's a fantastic legacy."

The Post Company also grew enormously as a business during Mrs. Graham's three decades of leadership. Revenue grew nearly twentyfold as the company acquired numerous new businesses and became a public corporation listed on the New York Stock Exchange.

On July 18, 2001, in its obituary, *The Washington Post* wrote: "After Nixon's resignation, the newspaper's role in unraveling the Watergate story produced, among other things, worldwide acclaim for Mrs. Graham and the paper, a Pulitzer Prize for meritorious public service, a Robert Redford movie based on the Woodward and Bernstein book *All the President's Men*—and discomfort as well as pleasure for the paper's publisher. With all the attention the *Post* was receiving, she feared that the staff might be distracted from its daily work, that the paper might become too taken with itself, 'that if your profile gets too high it will be a target.'"

Just a few months after the publication the of *HBR* special issue on leadership, on May 6, 2002, *The Wall Street Journal* ran an op-ed by Robert Bartley headlined "Businessmen in the Dock." The article lamented potential prosecution of Enron's Ken Lay, the resignation of the CEO of Arthur Andersen, the conviction of former Sotheby's chairman Alfred Taubman, and the Justice Department case against Bill Gates. *The Economist* of May 4 ran a cover reading "Fallen Idols: The Overthrow of Celebrity CEO's." "Business leaders," noted the story, "are being knocked off their pedestals faster than Communist heroes after the fall of the Berlin Wall."

The point is not that business leaders should be expected to be any less fallible than the rest of us. Every profession has its scoundrels. And an occupational hazard of leading is going where others have not gone before, which can sometimes mean crossing a line. But those who aspire to leadership should recognize that in addition to the very valuable skills of marketing, economic forecasting, and team building, one's leadership qualities are likely to be both enhanced and sustained by listening to one's own conscience as carefully as one listens to Wall Street or one's CFO.

Leaders are followed only if they know where they are going. Nothing undermines the confidence of an organization more than a leader who doesn't seem true to his or her own heart.

Another great example of conscience-driven leadership that proved successful beyond all expectation comes out of the Cuban missile crisis of 1962.

"I could not accept the idea that the United States would rain bombs on Cuba, killing thousands and thousands of civilians in a surprise attack. . . . We spent more time on this moral question during the first five days than on any other single matter," Robert Kennedy wrote later in his account of the crisis, *Thirteen Days*.

A memorandum from the State Department's deputy legal adviser, Leonard Meeker (quoted in Arthur Schlesinger, Jr.'s *Robert Kennedy and His Times*), explains: "The Attorney General . . . said there seemed to be three main possibilities . . . one was to do nothing, and that was unthinkable; another was an air strike; a third was a blockade. He thought it would be very, very difficult indeed for the President if the decision were to be for an air strike, with all the memory of Pearl Harbor and with all the implications this would have for us in whatever world there would be afterward. For 175 years we had not been that kind of country. A sneak attack was not in our traditions. Thousands of Cubans would be killed without warning, and a lot of Russians too. He favored *action,* to make known unmistakably the seriousness of United States determination to get the missiles out of Cuba, but he thought the action should allow the Soviets some room for maneuver to pull back from their over-extended position in Cuba."

Twelve days afterward, Kennedy recalled: "I said I just did not believe the President of the United States could order such a military operation. I said we were fighting for something more than just survival and that all our heritage and our ideals would be repugnant to such a sneak military attack."

The Joint Chiefs of Staff had planned and were advocating an air strike. They obviously had much greater military experience than Robert Kennedy. C. Douglas Dillon explained the influence of Bobby Kennedy's position. "I felt that I was at a real turning point in history. . . . The way Bobby Kennedy spoke was totally convincing to me. I knew then that we should not undertake a strike without warning."

The stakes had never been higher. Bobby Kennedy and his brother the president didn't have time to page through leadership books. Their strategic calculations about the intentions of the Soviets were savvy, but gambles nevertheless. What Bobby Kennedy did do was look inward to the values that'd he'd learned to be the values of the nation. Relying on conscience over command structure, his argument carried the day and led the United States along a path that averted the most serious threat of nuclear war our country has ever faced.

LEADING FROM THE HEART

THERE IS ANOTHER path to leadership. Instead of a reading light, it demands a stethoscope. For it is about listening to one's heart. By that I don't mean following one's emotions, but rather listening carefully to one's truest thoughts and values. It requires less external searching than internal exploration. It is less expensive and less time-consuming than the advice peddled for $22.95 in hardcover. It doesn't require mimicking the behaviors of coaches, queens, or Arctic explorers. In fact it demands the opposite. It requires looking within.

Nothing so inspires followers as the sure knowledge that their leader authentically believes in the course he or she is espousing, and moreover that the course is born of personal experience. Determining where to go by looking at one's conscience may be the shortest distance between two points.

The fall 2001 issue of *Leader to Leader* magazine includes an interview with a teacher and writer named Parker Palmer, author of *Let Your Life Speak* and *The Courage to Teach*. Palmer writes about the need for leaders to take an "inner journey." His thoughts more eloquently express some of what I have been aiming at in this chapter:

> Because the inner world is a source of reality and power as much as the outer world . . . I learned it from oppressed

people who have no power except inner power—and yet have created great social change. In our time we've seen the impact of people like Nelson Mandela, Rosa Parks, and Vaclav Havel, who found the courage to lead from their own deepest truths.

The best leaders work from a place of integrity in themselves, from their hearts. If they don't, they can't inspire trustful relationships. In the absence of trust, relationships fall apart. As the great jazz saxophonist Charlie Parker said: "If it ain't in your heart, it ain't in your horn." We can hear the horns everywhere, but if they're not being played from the heart, then certain negative consequences follow.

The leadership books I wrote about sarcastically a few pages ago all coax us into picking up someone else's horn. What a mockery this makes of harmony, of listening quietly for what is most authentic. If I've ever been effective as a leader at Share Our Strength, it has not been because I preached a course of action but because I shared a personal or professional experience that taught me something and that spoke to others.

It is an example of the kind of inner power that Parker Palmer talks about when he says:

> Look at history. Think for a moment about the lives of oppressed people around the world. These people have had no access to the tools of control and domination—like

money, status, or political clout—to work for change. The only power they have access to is inward.

But history shows time and again how people who might be regarded as "weak" have used the power of the human heart. History shows how they have taken hope and vision on the one hand and anger and fury on the other to create real and massive transformation. Whether we're talking about people of color or women or any other minority, no form of injustice would ever have been righted or transformed if it weren't for the fact that the human heart is a source of great power in the world.

As people draw nearer to that place within themselves, they start to feel the painful consequences that can come from leading from their hearts. But they also see that the consequences of not doing so are even more painful. Not doing so results in a divided life—behaving one way on the outside while believing or affirming something completely different on the inside. In human terms, that is a recipe for disaster.

How did Mandela, Havel and Parks decide to live "divided no more"—especially when they knew they would be severely punished if they acted from their deepest truths? I believe they all came to understand that no external punishment could possibly be greater than the punishment we impose on ourselves by conspiring in our own diminishment.

My friend Jeff Swartz could be counted on to put this in a biblical context:

You write about "inner journey," the voyage between the heart and the head, the connecting of the soul to the intellect and the sensory apparatus. Regarding this very point, Rabbi Samuels taught that "the distance between the Heavens and the earth is immense; to travel that distance is farther than from earth to Alpha Centauri, but it is a distance that can be bridged, by faithful practice of mitzvot. . . . What is daunting, then, is not the distance from here to the stars, or from where we stand to where we aspire—the voyage that is overwhelming to contemplate is the journey within, from the heart to the head (note the direction—not from the carefully thought through, but from the deeply felt). . . ."

The Babylonian Talmud recounts the story of Rabban Gamliel, the Nasi (Prince) who ruled the Sanhedrin (the Great Court) in this period of exile. In his city, there was one academy, one place where all who wished to learn and transform themselves "had" to study. When Rabban Gamliel was Nasi, he appointed a gatekeeper and decreed, "Any student whose inside is not as his outside, may not enter here."

The gatekeeper had essentially two choices—admit everyone, or no one. He chose the latter. And so many, many seekers were sent away. Their journey was re-routed—to where? The Talmud says nothing. . . . These lonely seekers hadn't the courage you write about.

Of a few seekers, however, the Gemara relates that no gatekeeper could keep them from their journey. If not through the front door, then through the back door, or through a second floor window—they would make their way in, because they sought the truth that was locked in the academy; they had to dive into the sacred text, not merely to learn others' ways or others' answers, but to be informed, in order to build their own model of living purposefully. They were bound to live their quest.

VII

The Art of Conscience

The ancient commission of the writer has not changed. He is charged with exposing our many grievous faults and failures, with dredging up to the light our dark and dangerous dreams for the purpose of improvement. Furthermore, the writer is delegated to declare and to celebrate man's proven capacity for greatness of heart and spirit—for gallantry in defeat—for courage, compassion and love. In the endless war against weakness and despair, these are the bright rally flags of hope and of emulation.

—JOHN STEINBECK

THE OBLIGATION NOT TO LOOK AWAY

MUCH OF OUR most acclaimed literature celebrates individuals who put their conscience above every other expediency. In *To Kill a Mockingbird,* Atticus Finch stares down a lynch mob to protect and defend a man unjustly accused. In *A Man for All Seasons,* Thomas More, unwilling to sanction any defiance of papal authority on behalf of King Henry VIII, resigned from the chancellorship in 1532 and refused to take an oath of supremacy, asserting that Parliament did not have the right to usurp papal authority in favor of the king, even though he knew it meant certain execution. Four hundred years later he was canonized by the Roman Catholic Church.

From John Steinbeck's *The Grapes of Wrath* to Upton Sinclair's *The Jungle,* books have called our attention to issues otherwise easy to ignore. Movies ranging from *The Graduate* to *Star Wars* celebrate the individual who resists entreaties to take the easy or conventionally popular path rather than the road less traveled.

Henry David Thoreau used the power of the essay to make the case for civil disobedience that was the foundation for the efforts of Gandhi and Martin Luther King.

The arts yield many other manifestations of the obligation not to look away.

When Share Our Strength friend and supporter Jeff Swartz, CEO of Timberland, came to meet with me recently, he brought a book as a gift.

Jeff arrived from Los Angeles, where he'd just visited the Getty Museum's exhibition about Depression-era photographer Dorothea Lange. The book contained her photographs of bread lines, waterfront strikes, and migrant workers, which have had such a profound impact on the development of modern documentary photography. Her work was used at the time as evidence of the need for government action to assist hungry Americans.

The arc of the book's visual narrative is pronounced and painful to witness. Lange's early work, from the 1920s through the beginning of the '30s, consists of portraits and pictures of family and friends. Eyes shine and sparkle. There are children at play, swimming in a California creek, bathed in sunlight, as innocent as they are naked. They seem to have not a care in the world. It's like a scene Gauguin could have painted. There are smiles, notable only because we will not see a smile again in this book, not even once, in the two hundred pages that depict life after 1930.

With the onset of the Depression, Lange's work takes a turn. The lightness of childhood is replaced with the weight of worry. The expressions of the children in her pictures are no longer of wonder, but of wondering, about where they will come to rest, when they will eat, why their migration takes them past people who have so much more. It was as if Lange realized that a camera had another use, that it could and must be put to a larger purpose. In this way Lange was not only a talented photographer but also a moral entrepreneur, helping to introduce a new morality into her profession, and a sense of social responsibility that generations of documentary photographers to follow would come to embrace.

Her black-and-white photography accentuates the starkness of the farmer stranded and stalled in a ditch, the cloth roof of his truck in tatters and every stain visible on his sleeve. Or of the woman on the high plains of the Texas panhandle, one hand on her brow, the other supporting her neck, a wedding ring with faded promise glinting from the shadows. The book's cover photo is of a young mother with two scruffy children, one of whom nurses from a Coke bottle. Their eyes are wary. Having a photographer aiming her lens at them must be out of the ordinary, and if there is one thing they've learned in their short lives it is that "out of the ordinary" doesn't break their way.

Dorothea Lange is about people. No landscapes here, no still lifes either. In the entire book, I found less than half a dozen photos in which her camera was not trained on human beings. Like the painter Jacob Lawrence, Lange documents migration. Hers are photographs of people in the midst of the most harrowing journey of their lives. When she died at seventy-five, fellow photographer Eugene Smith eulogized the "belief in the worth of life she has so evidenced in her work."

Each picture can be appreciated for itself, but spend enough time with the entire collection and patterns slowly emerge, like dawn breaking, patterns of what can be seen and not seen. For example, one thing you don't see in Lange's work is whole families. In 264 pages there are only four photographs of children with both their mother and father. Some of the most compelling, like "Migrant Mother" and the cover photo, "Mother and Children on the Road in Tulelake," are of moms with their children pulled close to them. But there are also a few of only dads with the kids. It's as if Lange is saying that food is not the only thing missing here. Take away something as basic as a family's meals, and the very concept of family, so central to our whole society, starts to fracture.

Lange literally looked up to many of her subjects, shooting them from below, adding a heroic dimension, as if to insist on the heroism of human beings who struggle and prevail. That was her doing. But notice how many of the people in Dorothea Lange's pictures, including the now iconic "Migrant Mother," are looking up and off into the distance, toward the horizon. Only rarely are they distracted, preoccupied, looking down or away. Most have lifted their gaze. Searching. Almost expectantly. Because they are American, they remain hopeful that something better is coming. They know that hunger is not the natural order of things. It's as if they are waiting for the cavalry to arrive. Or maybe they are just looking for you and me.

I wonder whether the same photos could be taken today. I wonder if those who are hungry would still look up, expectantly, even if naively, seeking and waiting for something better. Unfortunately, tragically, hunger has nearly become the natural order today.

Our first obligation, the one that cannot be excused, is to see, to bear witness, to pause and not look away.

I am only telling you what Jeff Swartz's gift told me, what Dorothea Lange tells all of us.

TWENTY-FIRST-CENTURY MONUMENTS

EVEN STANDING UPON it, you might never know that the patch of grass near the Hudson River is the new Irish Hunger Memorial. Part of its power is that it makes you work to ficure out what it is trying to say. There are no pictures of starving children, no likenesses of victims, no real evidence of what hunger does, how it feels, or the toll it takes. Here the suffering can only be imagined, which is always the challenge for those spared it. Or it may be beyond our imagining, further increasing our respect for it. Only after leaving, days afterward, frankly, did I realize the memorial had been gently but insistently asking whether we are willing to do the work it takes to understand hunger and to end it.

During the week that designs were unveiled to redevelop and memorialize the property in lower Manhattan where the World Trade Center towers once stood, the already completed Irish Hunger Memorial was being unveiled just two blocks from the deep cavern that is Ground Zero.

Ireland lost more than two million of its people to starvation and emigration between 1845 and 1852, when blight killed off the Irish potato crop. A half acre of green sod flown in from Ireland replicates an Irish hillside. It is threaded with paths, native flora, and fallow potato furrows. Set against the sky-scraping towers of the financial district, it is a most unusual tribute.

The landscape rests on a giant slab of fossilized Irish limestone tilted up toward the sky, like a flying saucer dropped in from space. Its highest ridge offers a view of the Statue of Liberty and Ellis Island, not unlike the view so many Irish emigrants had as they approached the shores they believed waves of hunger could not reach.

At the memorial's center sits a Famine-era stone cottage donated by a family in County Mayo and painstakingly reconstructed. It has no roof, like the cottages of farmers who tore the thatches off to prove destitution and qualify for relief. The surrounding sod is dotted with thirty-two large stones, one from each of Ireland's counties, and the kind of plants often found growing in fallow fields: bearberry, ling heather, foxglove, and burnet rose.

Unlike most memorials that fit their settings with perfect aesthetic symmetry, as do those in Washington, D.C., this memorial is jarring in its dissonance: a field of green against the gray steel towers of the urban landscape, a half-built cottage across the street from the comfort of an Embassy Suites hotel, the fallow furrows of potato fields visible from the windows of corporate dining rooms replete with America's finest bounty. It's as if the memorial were sited to make the point that hunger doesn't fit here, that it has no place, that even so much as a reminder of it should make us stop and look twice.

The memorial also invites reflection on those still hungry around the world today. The walls of its base are lined with glass-covered statements about the Irish famine from that period, as well as current calls to action:

> 'Tis hard to argue starvation into quiet, to bid hunger to be silent. They are both spirits of riot, and clamor and tumult are their mode of warfare. (Editorial in the Waterford *Freeman*, October 7, 1846)

Wedged into the shadow of American Express headquarters and the Stock Exchange, in the heart of American capitalism, the Irish Hunger Memorial exemplifies how America's great public monuments have changed. The way they've changed speaks volumes about the collective conscience of America today.

When I moved to Washington, D.C., in 1977 there were three memorials, along with the White House and the Capitol, that all tourists came to see: the Lincoln Memorial, the Jefferson Memorial, and the Washington Monument. Their colossal, majestic structures make presidents into gods. The gleaming white marble affirms an unassailable purity.

I often wonder what it means to live in an age that no longer produces leaders to whom such monuments are built. The Lincoln Memorial was designed to resemble a Greek temple, its thirty-six Doric columns each forty-four feet high. Is there a man or woman of our era deemed worthy of that today? Modern presidents must wonder too. Rather than leave anything to chance, they now build their own memorials, under the euphemism of "presidential libraries."

The Vietnam War changed the memorial business. It so tarnished our leaders, and so traumatized the rest of us, that monument momentum shifted from those who made big decisions to those who suffered their consequences. In the case of Vietnam, that was all of us. Part of the genius of the Vietnam Veterans Memorial Wall, in addition to its fifty-seven thousand engraved names, is that you can't get close to it without seeing yourself reflected in the haunting black marble. The memorial is also about you.

The Holocaust Memorial Museum followed suit, and more recently the Korean War Veterans Memorial. Memorials are no longer about leaders we know and revere. Instead it is the anonymous and unknown victims who merit our pilgrimage.

Just as acts of conscience change the world, so the Irish Hunger Memorial and the Vietnam Memorial show us how the world changes when we turn a deaf ear and a blind eye to conscience. As *New York Times* art critic Roberta Smith noted of the Irish Hunger Memorial, "it is a figureless terrain in which the viewer stands in for the heroic statue." It's as if at the end of the twentieth century we realized that the responsibility for solving our most challenging problems no longer lies with our leaders alone, but also, even principally, with ourselves.

Like the Vietnam Memorial, the Irish Hunger Memorial is not one of those forbidding "Keep Off," "Do Not Touch," "Do Not Climb On" kinds of places. It is hands-on. You walk across it, in furrows where potato plants should grow but don't and didn't. Brian Tolle, the artist who designed it, explained in an interview: "It will be constantly changing. The tradition of the monument is something that is unchanging, unyielding, that continues to persevere as the world changes around it. You know what happens—eventually people just forget about it because attitudes change, the event was so long ago that it's just a block of stone in the park. The Hunger Memorial is something that can go in either direction. It can be neglected, in which case it gets more wild. Or, I'm dead and the architects are dead and somebody says, 'It would look nice if we had tulips planted there.' It will reflect changing attitudes and cultural shifts."

Hunger still exists, not just across the ocean but a taxi ride away. A million and a half New Yorkers, one third of them children, will turn to soup kitchens for sustenance sometime this year. Few of us actually see it, and building a memorial a century and a half later will be little consolation. Walking away from the Irish Hunger Memorial leaves us grateful for the eloquent reminder, but also chagrined that we need it. We know most of life's injustices are not as glaringly visible. Indeed, invisibility, darkness, and ignorance are what permit injustices to flourish. Men and women of conscience must seek them out where they are less obvious and less convenient and less comfortable to find. The obligation of men and women of conscience is not just to react or respond when moved, but to seek out what will move us.

JOURNEY OF CONSCIENCE

I'D BEEN COUNTING the days until the Jacob Lawrence show opened at the Phillips Collection near Dupont Circle. Lawrence is one of the epic storytellers of American history, and his stories are always about a journey. He was born in Harlem in 1917 and died in 2000. He was the first American artist trained in and by the black community in Harlem and the first to receive sustained support from mainstream art museums outside the black community.

The show included two hundred paintings, but it was the sixty panels of the Migration series that had captured and held my imagination since I had learned of them years earlier. In these sixty paintings, completed in 1940, Lawrence conveyed the struggle and strife of the massive African American population shift from rural South to industrial North.

Each panel was a straightforward depiction of a distinct element of the migration: the lines and luggage at the train stations, crops left to dry and spoil under the southern sun, blacks at a polling place voting for the first time. The paintings showed a dark side too: the lynchings, child labor, and lack of education that drove blacks from the South. Lawrence painted in bright, bold primary colors and simple geometric shapes. Like his previous series on Frederick Douglass and Harriet Tubman, these paintings were accompanied by a simple narrative that Lawrence had written in advance, such as "They were very poor" or "The trains were packed continually with migrants."

At first the paintings seemed almost childlike. For example, panel number 10 was of a man and woman sitting at a brown table, bare except for an empty bowl and plate in front of them. They sit motionless, hands hanging at their sides, and it's as if they had so little to eat that it was gone before the painter could capture them eating it. Or number 58, of three girls standing at a huge blue blackboard, in simple dresses of yellow, ochre, and pale blue. The right arm of each stretches to write a numeral with white chalk, each one higher than the next. When the sixty panels were viewed as a whole, the paintings were not childlike, but their starkness and strength made them powerful enough for a child to understand.

These sixty panels rarely appear together. They were first exhibited in December 1941 by Edith Halpert, daughter of Jewish immigrants from Odessa, Russia. Her field of expertise was merchandising, learned first in her parents' candy store and later from working in department stores. An aspiring artist, she had planned a major project to wake the segregated New York art world to contemporary African American artists. Pearl Harbor was attacked the day before her gala opening. The show collapsed, but she went forward with the Migration series.

Halpert brought the paintings to editors she knew at *For-*

tune magazine. Henry Luce and other business executives had a strong interest in images of blacks working effectively in northern factories as the nation geared up for war production. So in November 1941, *Fortune* published a full-color spread of almost half of the Migration series, an early example of business interests aligning with a social justice message.

In 1942 the Museum of Modern Art in New York and the Phillips Collection in D.C. both expressed interest in owning the sixty panels of the Migration series. As a compromise they were divided in half, the even-numbered paintings going to one museum and the odd-numbered to the other.

When the series is viewed as a whole, patterns emerge. In most of the paintings the migrants have their backs to us as they stand facing the train station, or the polling booth, or the judge in court. We rarely see their faces and almost never see their eyes. The business of seeing is our job, a task that has been assigned to us. But it was Lawrence's job to make us see. This is one consequence of an act of conscience: it makes us see, feel, be aware. It reverberates through time and reminds us of our own responsibilities.

The brilliance of these paintings is that they point toward the future as well as the past. One hundred years later the struggles of great migrations are still being waged around us every day. The fourteen Mexicans who died in the Arizona desert were a part of them. Or the two million Afghans who have crossed into Pakistan's refugee camps, the Sudanese fleeing civil war, even the Ethiopians walking hours a day for water. But they are fleeting images, quickly pushed aside by whatever passes for the next day's news, whether J. Lo's romance or suicide bombers in the Mideast.

Lawrence had something more permanent in mind. He painted on wooden panels instead of canvas or paper, and in bright primary colors that haven't faded for half a century. His pictures are so spare they are almost empty. No frills or fashions, no other clues about the migrants' lives. Their lives are defined by this journey. The figures in the paintings are African American, but their journey also belongs to other times and other places. The same quest for food and freedom that drove Lawrence's migrants, the same search for safety and peace, is still being waged on every continent of the globe.

Jacob Lawrence used his paintbrush to swear us in as witnesses. His will was that we should see. His was not the work of protest marches or hunger strikes, not the business of getting arrested or standing in front of tanks. His work took place more quietly, in a studio filled with paper and wood and jars of paint. His contribution came not in a celebrated moment that captured the world's attention, but with diligence and discipline over the course of almost seventy years.

With sixty paintings spread through half a dozen rooms of the Phillips Collection, Lawrence asks us not only to see but to move with the migration, to follow it, to be part of it. It's as if he's issued a challenge of sorts, not to be complacent, to look around the next corner, to search for the great tides of history and to know them, and to know ourselves.

Walker Evans, who chronicled much of the same historic period, but in photographs, once told his students: "Stare. It is the way to educate your eye, and more. Stare, pry, listen, eavesdrop. Die knowing something. You are not here long."

The last panel Lawrence painted is filled with men, women, and children near a train track, more crowded than almost any of the others in the series. The narrative he wrote to accompany this last panel is "And the migrants kept coming." Somehow Lawrence knew they always would.

CONSCIENCE AND COMPLICITY

I TOOK THE train to New York to look at thirty-eight photographs. They are not famous or popular photographs. They probably never will be. In fact they are thirty-eight photographs that no other person came to see during the time I was there. They were not being bought or sold. Commerce is not their purpose. Conscience is.

I'd read about the pictures in *The New York Times*. They were taken by Brazilian photojournalist Sebastio Selgado as part of a campaign called "The End of Polio." Selgado traveled to India, Pakistan, Somalia, Sudan, and Congo to tell the polio eradication story.

The African backdrops look like places I've been. The dusty road and rubble of brick are familiar. So are the gaunt, deliberate people, and the paradox of reticence and curiosity in their dark eyes.

When I saw the story in the newspaper I wanted to see the pictures for myself. The idea of ending a disease, eradicating it forever, is a powerful one, inspiring but seemingly impossible, not unlike Share Our Strength's goal of ending hunger. As with polio, we know the solution to hunger, but given the enormity of the task, and the complex obstacles that block the path, there is a question as to whether we have the will and the long-term vision to sustain it.

I also saw the direct connection between these photos and how acts of conscience can change the world. That is the aim of documentary photography. Our eyes are the windows of our conscience. What we see becomes a part of us, imprinted on a neuron as surely as if injected into a vein. What is witnessed can't be erased or taken back. When an image we've taken in clashes with our sense of who we are or who we want to be, whether as individuals or society as a whole, it's our conscience that makes itself heard.

The Selgado photos hung on the walls of two small rooms on the second floor of an office building on Twenty-third Street, near Madison Square. The rooms themselves served as offices for the photography publisher *Aperture*. To see all of the photos you had to walk around a few staffers working at their desks, and occasionally squeeze past them.

About half of Selgado's thirty-eight photos depict children in various settings receiving a few drops of oral vaccine. In each picture a small child is held in the tight grip of an adult, a dropper poised over its mouth by a health worker. The children are as fearful as if facing a long hypodermic needle. Given the unfamiliarity of the procedure, the parents are too. In one of the pictures, the mother's face twists in a pained, sympathetic grimace, even though her child is only receiving two drops of liquid from a plastic dropper. In other pictures, parents stare piercingly into the lens, betraying a skepticism about cameraman and vaccination alike.

In many of the photos, four or five adults surround the child. They are there for support, or to hold down arms and legs if necessary, or simply to satisfy their curiosity about such an unusual event. They have scant knowledge of the medicine, but have gathered in awe of that unknowable power that ensures that life will triumph over the crippling pain and death they've previously known. That is what they see unleashed with each squeeze of the dropper. Through Selgado's camera, we see it too.

Selgado's photos differ from the traditional documentary imagery that dramatizes despair and provokes outrage. He wants to emphasize solutions and show that the eradication of polio is within reach. It was hoped this would generate the energy and commitment for the push to raise the final $275 million needed to complete the "End of Polio" campaign.

The photos in the rest of the exhibition convey just

how enormous is the task, and how many unimaginable obstacles must be overcome. They also document the ingenuity brought to bear in far reaches of our planet where it might not be expected.

One picture is of a checkpoint set up on the Congo River where every passing canoe is checked for a child under five. On National Immunization Days in India, no train may leave the station until every child has shown proof of vaccination. In Somalia, the Juba River is the border between two clans, neither of which will accept the vaccine except from their own health workers, so the refrigerated boxes must be handed off from one group on a raft to another on shore. For the children of nomads following their camels through Somalia, one finger is marked with ink so other health workers will know they received the vaccine.

When it comes to eradicating such an ancient scourge, good is not good enough. The campaign must be relentless and thorough. If just one child slips through the cracks, just one child on either of two vast continents, it could mean the difference between the ongoing agony of the disease and a world in which it no longer exists except in laboratory test tubes . . . and photographs.

In 1988, 350,000 children around the world were paralyzed by polio, a highly infectious disease which the world has long had the vaccine to prevent. In 2001 there were just 480 cases, and international health groups vaccinated more than 575 million children. Polio principally affects children under the age of five. There is no cure, only prevention. Four doses of oral polio vaccine protect a child for life. It is likely to be the second disease, after smallpox, to be eradicated as the result of a sustained global campaign.

What is all the more amazing about this is you know that someone, at some task force or committee meeting, must have raised his hand and said: "Wait a minute. This will never work. We'd have to stop every canoe on the Congo River." And someone must have stood up at some board meeting and said, "We'll never be able to do this. We'd have to stop every train before it leaves the station all across India."

But they weren't working from the scarcity model, which says, "Here is what you have; what can you do with it?" Rather, they worked backward from a vision of what they believed was necessary to get the job done and save lives, and said, "Okay, what do we need to do to achieve this?"

Documentary photographs like Selgado's do more than make us think. They make us complicit. Once we've seen what the photographer has seen we are left with a choice: do something or do nothing. The pictures are no longer just objects on the walls. They are within us and we carry them wherever we go.

In this way these pictures increase self-awareness as much as they do public awareness. The way we react to them tells us more about who we are. They reinforce the notion that each of us has a choice to make about acting on what we see, and that our first responsibility is just that: to see. "I hope the person who visits my exhibitions, and the person who comes out, is not quite the same," Selgado explains.

Images lead to action. Some photos cause funds to be raised. Others might lead to congressional hearings. Eventually public consensus builds, presidents speak, laws are passed. And the world changes.

VIII

Conscience Is Global

I know how people are, with their habits of mind. Most will sail through from cradle to grave with a conscience clean as snow. It's easy to point at other men, conveniently dead, starting with the ones who first scooped up mud from riverbanks to catch the scent of a source. Why, Dr. Livingstone, I presume, wasn't he the rascal! He and all the profiteers who've since walked out on Africa as a husband quits a wife, leaving her with her naked body curled around the emptied-out mine of her womb. I know people. Most have no earthly notion of the price of a snow-white conscience.

—BARBARA KINGSOLVER,
The Poisonwood Bible

WHAT'S AT STAKE

IT IS THE morning after September 11, and I'm standing in the Pentagon's south parking lot. The smoke has cleared but not the acrid smell. From where I stand at the very base of the building, the men walking and working on its roof seem small, like miniature toy soldiers. The building is that massive. Cranes pick at its gash like vultures tearing into a wound.

There's no running and shouting anymore. Instead the parking lot that surrounds the Pentagon looks like the site of a convention, or a public safety flea market. Tents have been erected. Salvation Army and Red Cross vehicles bearing license plates from Virginia, Maryland, North and South Carolina, Texas, Tennessee, and a dozen other states are parked side by side with local ambulances. A mobile McDonald's has been erected, complete with golden arches. Enough Gatorade has been stacked on pallets to quench the thirst of the entire armed forces. Volunteers resting on folding chairs find shade, share stories, exchange business cards. It is possible to forget that a hundred and eighty bodies lie trapped beneath the rubble just yards away. But not for long.

I came to perform the smallest of chores: hauling five hundred pounds of charcoal briquettes from the back of my Jeep to the huge grill constructed by Share Our Strength's friends at Tyson Foods. The plant manager who supervises six hundred employees at their Berlin, Maryland, factory brought his team members and an eighteen-wheeler loaded with chicken. They are going through more than four tons of chicken a day, feeding as many as 2,500 rescuers and volunteers. Share Our Strength facilitated their participation here, though nothing could have kept them away. When they run over to express their gratitude for having some role to play, I know just how they feel.

Beyond managing grief, the toughest challenge for those

of us who are not firemen, doctors, or ironworkers has been finding a way to help. Confronted with a catastrophe of this scale, it's almost impossible to do anything that feels significant. So the small things count. I stack the briquettes with extra care.

The headlines shout what our hearts already knew: The world has changed. But we're left alone to figure out what that means for each of us and what it means for the work we do. Twice that week I was told: "The issue isn't hunger and poverty anymore." How can we expect our work to be a priority when America is engaged in what the president has called the first war of the twenty-first century?

America unleashed the greatest demonstration of military might in our history. But military might cannot make a nation strong. It can only protect the strengths already existing within. A concerted campaign to end terrorism will take years, and requires America to stand united. True national unity means more than a chorus of support for military action. That is merely the minimum requirement. A sustained campaign also requires unity of experience, ability, purpose, and outlook.

A nation rent by deep divisions between black and white, rich and poor, is not sufficiently united. Children weakened by malnutrition or missed immunizations, endangered by dilapidated housing or violent schools, are not what a nation defending its borders can afford. During peace and prosperity such conditions challenge our notion of justice. During war they threaten our very security. (This was why Congress created the school lunch program after World War II.) Non-profit organizations addressing these issues, and the philanthropy that supports them, must not take a backseat now, but instead redouble their efforts.

A producer at CBS told me that the news-gathering efforts after September 11 were the most challenging, remarkable, and rewarding time of his career, "but I would trade it all in for the chance to be down at Ground Zero and lift just one brick off the pile."

It doesn't take away from the courage of those who run into burning buildings to suggest that another kind of courage should be acknowledged in America today. It is the courage to volunteer in a community where others fear to tread. It is the courage to donate even more than before. It is the courage to share one's strength by coaching, teaching, or mentoring someone who may not have the advantages we've had. Tackling America's internal challenges with the same success we hope for abroad will take more than acts of courage. It will take dedicating each of our lives to making real the principles of equality and opportunity that have always made America worth fighting for.

If there was a shortage of American heroes before September 11, it was in perception only. An entire industry devoted to saving lives has come to maturity in communities across the country. It can be found not just in firehouses but in food banks and foster homes, not just at the United Way but in the way mentors, tutors, teachers, and others have cared for those left behind during the years of prosperity that made many Americans feel invincible.

Two years after September 11, more than half of the books on the *New York Times* nonfiction best-seller list were remembrances or analyses of September 11. From Lisa Beamer's *Let's Roll* to the CBS News compilation called *What We Saw,* much has been written.

I will chance one observation I haven't seen elsewhere that underscores the reach and relevance of conscience in these perilous times: In the aftermath of September 11, Americans have come not only to expect but also to demand more from one another. This higher standard has indirectly but unmistakably made itself felt across all of the disciplines that intersect our daily lives, from business and politics to religion and sports. As a result, previously unassailable institutions have been leveled as surely as the Twin Towers. The treachery of the few who acted unconscionably that September morning spawned a new premium on conscientious and ethical conduct for the rest of us, the way scarcity in a few oil sheiks' petroleum reserves creates a premium on gasoline.

Ethical and conscience-related dramas revolving around age-old themes of greed, lust, and betrayal came to dominate the national conversation. Outside of terrorism and Iraq, the greatest news coverage in the year after September 11 was reserved for the corporate accounting scandals that mushroomed like an atomic cloud at Enron, WorldCom, Tyco, and other companies. They've made an oxymoron of "corporate ethics" and all but shattered confidence in the corporate executives we had come to glorify for their success and leadership. During the economic boom that transformed the United States throughout much of the 1990s, corporate CEOs became our new cultural icons. We looked to them not only to create wealth but also to write books, offer wisdom on leadership, and inspire other enterprises to succeed like their own.

The other major national news story that preceded this one by a few months was the Catholic Church's epidemic of pedophile priests. It put some of the church's most respected leaders on the defensive and in some cases under intense pressure to resign. Only some of the anger has been directed toward the accused. Much of it has been directed toward the accuseds' superiors, particularly those who knew of specific abuses and looked the other way. The problem is not a new one to the Catholic Church, but the virulence of the public's refusal to tolerate it any longer is unprecedented.

Of course none of those involved in these stories had anything to do with the events of September 11. Nor did September 11 affect the timing, severity, or scale of their misdeeds. That is not the relationship I'm suggesting. Crimes are committed all the time. Lines are crossed. Mistakes are made. Greed is as old as the Bible. There have always been predators and prey. But the real issue in each of these stories, what gave public fascination its staying power, is that those at the center of each story were expected to know better, and indeed did know better. The drama of these stories is in the betrayal—in what Arthur Miller described in a section of his memoir about *The Crucible* and the Salem witch trials as "what they called then the breaking of charity with one another."

So while such events would have been headline news in any year, in the year following September 11 they became more than that. These and other revelations resonated with average Americans in ways they previously did not. They resonated with a power and a fury that led to far-reaching action. Long-overdue reforms suddenly became inevitable, business as usual gave way to a new order. There were finally wide-ranging reforms in corporate governance, through passage of the Sarbanes-Oxley Act, in accounting procedures, in church policy. Events like the corporate debacles and church scandals proved directly related to September 11, through the standards by which we judged them and the actions that followed in their wake.

If anything encouraging emerged from the ash and rubble of the World Trade Center towers—and because we are Americans we searched for that as determinedly as we searched for survivors—it was that the instincts of so many people were so good. Character was not forged in this crucible so much as revealed, and what we saw was widely viewed as cause for solemn but proud celebration. Not just the police and firefighters whose heroics have been so well documented and recognized, but the journalists, students, restaurateurs, blood donors, financial contributors, and other volunteers in countless communities near to and far from Ground Zero who over the course of the year found some way to make a contribution.

Having witnessed citizenship at that level, why would we go back to settling for something less? Having claimed the high ground of generosity and selflessness, why would we retreat? Having watched so many labor so valiantly to raise the bar of what it means to be a conscientious citizen, who could be expected to stand by silently and watch it get knocked back down a peg, whether by Ken Lay or Cardinal Law?

We have come to expect more from one another. A nation threatened will no longer tolerate the mischief or miscreants from which it once looked the other way, any more than a once-profitable business gone bankrupt can continue to tolerate waste, fraud, or those on its payroll who don't perform. Cutting corners no longer comes at the expense only of the victims, but at the expense of all of us.

Right and wrong are more black and white than the gray they often seemed before the towers fell. Against this backdrop, the betrayals represented by dishonest business leaders and predatory priests, though not new in the annals of crime, are no longer tolerable. With that new clarity of vision, those seen as diluting American values are seen as diluting American strength.

To those who wish America ill, this might give them pause were it not so difficult for them to see. Like the elegant spiderweb stretching between two evergreens outside my front door, it is all the more dangerous to the unsuspecting for being so well camouflaged and so underestimated. America's new collective conscience may be our ultimate secret weapon, self-modernizing, ever-renewing, our natural and best defense.

CONSCIENCE ACROSS GENERATIONS

ON THE MONDAY following the September 11 terrorist attacks on New York and Washington, *The Christian Science Monitor* published a special edition of its daily newspaper. Half of the front page was a photo of the Twin Towers wreckage. The headline that day, which now seems almost clichéd, was "A Changed World." In the upper left-hand corner, where it runs each issue, is the paper's motto, almost embarrassingly quaint if not tragically anachronistic: "To injure no man, but to bless all mankind."

This special edition was filled with color photographs capturing world reaction to the devastating loss of innocent lives: the FBI director and the attorney general standing at the Department of Justice lectern, a British policeman carrying bouquets of flowers past the U.S. embassy, German construction workers in yellow hard hats observing a moment of silence. The images were riveting, even if predictable.

One photo I could not have predicted. On page 13 there is a picture of six young men of high school age, dressed in black T-shirts and camouflage pants. They are waving American flags and holding a large handmade sign that says "Honk for the USA" in bold red, white, and blue letters. They are clustered like bowling pins, one tall one centered in front and the others wedged into formation behind him. Three of them are shouting, mouths open wide, like newborn chicks waiting to be fed. They are outdoors, at a busy intersection near the Lincoln Memorial in Washington, D.C. The still-green foliage of a large tree spreads out high above them, as if protectively. Though they are dressed in the uniform of highly skilled soldiers participating in special operations, they are still just teenage boys, well shy of enlistment age.

One of the boys, his close-cropped hair peeking out from under a baseball cap, has both hands aloft, his fingers forming a V, not for peace, as was once meant, too long ago for him even to be aware of, but instead for victory. His mouth is open wide, in the middle of a shout. Although the photo does not convey what he is saying, it can't fail to convey his determination to make himself heard. Having found his voice and a reason to use it, he assumes his place in a lineage he doesn't know exists.

The picture of this boy shares the page with a better-known photo of President George W. Bush standing atop the rubble at Ground Zero, one arm around a fireman, the other arm extended to hold a large megaphone. He assures Americans that our nation will prevail and that justice will be served. He too intends to make himself heard.

Each in his own way, the president and the boy are acting

on raw instinct. Though of different generations, they will be forever bound by their memory of this unprecedented moment. Each has surfaced in the center of a recently attacked city, drawn by and paying homage to the powerful symbols at hand. Each in his own way will attach importance to these photographs memorializing where they were and what they were doing. The president, of course, is in the newspaper almost every day. The boy has never been. He is my son Zach, two weeks shy of his sixteenth birthday.

The affairs of the nation and the affairs of my teenage son intersect under only the rarest of circumstances. Solar eclipses are more frequent. The president's schedule typically bears little resemblance to Zach's. Our republic is the better for that. No president could devote so much time to video games and still make it to National Security Council meetings.

The preoccupations of a teenage boy are many and varied but rarely include whatever headlines dominate *The New York Times* or *The Washington Post*. Headlines are usually no more relevant to Zach than the classified ads in Istanbul's daily paper. It hasn't been for lack of trying on my part. Each morning on the drive to school I actually pull over for a few minutes to look at the newspapers with him. At seven-thirty, halfway through our forty-minute ride, we switch the radio from his favorite rap station to National Public Radio, ensuring equal opportunity for each of us to be annoyed.

Zach's great fortune is to be a typical middle-class teenager. This may be the closest thing we have to royalty in

America. Like any member of royalty he is permitted to live his life parallel to the real world, blissfully oblivious to hardship or struggle. His world is one of sporting events and entertainments, hockey games, Friday-night movies, girlfriends, free music (on the Internet), and an allowance that bears little relation to the performance of official duties. He is chauffeured most places and often accompanied by ever-watchful and extremely protective bodyguards (his mother and me). Even parents who go to great lengths, as Zach's have, to ensure that their children are not spoiled rarely triumph over the prevailing culture.

As everything else changed on September 11, this changed too. During that week, for the first time, however briefly, the president and Zach found themselves sharing the same preoccupation. In a way, each had been awakened to a new sense of himself. It's been said that George Bush, often underestimated in the first months of his first term, discovered the purpose of his presidency, perhaps the purpose of his life, on September 11. That was not what Zach discovered. But what he did discover is that there are times to be purposeful. That there are times one lifts one's voice to express more than his or her own wants and needs. That there are moments beyond the very moment in which one lives and that what we say and do can affect the quality of those moments.

Three days after the attack, Zach and his eleventh-grade classmates at the Washington Waldorf School drove to an evening vigil being held between the Lincoln Memorial and the Capitol. This stretch of geography has long been America's favorite venue for protest marches, demonstrations, rallies, and vigils. Civil rights, gay rights, pro-war, anti-war. The Mall has seen it all. Think of it as America's premier political stage. Just as Carnegie Hall is the stage for classical performance, or Lincoln Center for jazz, the Mall is America's stage for expressing grievances of any kind. And as with any other dramatic stage there are established procedures for reserving it, precautions for protecting it, and press boxes for covering it.

In the aftermath of September 11, Americans young and old had been glued to their television sets virtually around the clock for days on end. Now they were beginning to come out and come together. Many of them were coming down to the Mall. Their reasons varied: to grieve, to seek solace in numbers, to overcome the feeling of being powerless in the face of such previously unimagined horror.

Later, when I asked Zach whose idea it had been to go down to the Mall, he answered, "I dunno," and I'm sure he meant it. Accountability among teenage boys is impossible to establish. A pack mentality prevails. Ideas travel mysteriously, almost contagiously, through phrases, grunts, and looks. The ambiguity of teenage planning is as natural and comfortable to kids as it is mysterious and uncomfortable to their parents. What was important to me—understanding the genesis of the impulse—was neither important nor interesting to him.

Having never before taken part in an event like the vigil on the Mall, Zach assumed the idea to be wholly original. He was flushed with the excitement of being part of it, and the energy and urgency of the crowd and the police and the cameramen had become his energy and urgency too. It wasn't an original idea, of course. But the experience was a new one to him—if only for the independence he enjoyed driving into town with his friends, straight toward the center of the action. I can only imagine the impression that the enormous crowd there must have made on him. Children naturally lack context, historic or otherwise.

The context Zach lacked was that far from being original, he is the third generation of Shores over the past half century to demonstrate on the Capitol grounds and Mall. This great American tradition has been his family's tradition as well. That's not to glorify any of our roles. We were all bit players, though at a time, I like to think, when bit players were just what was called for. History would have moved with or without any of us. We were hardly central to the proceedings. But we were there. Making ourselves heard. The mystery at the heart of democracy, and the essence of its persuasive power, is never knowing precisely where the tipping point is, not being able to prove conclusively which vote put a candidate over the top, which voice made the chorus compelling, which protester created enough of a crowd to draw the media—and so each one is equally vital, equally important. In this way Zach's instinct was right.

He was at the center of things. As was everyone else at the Mall.

The next day, as he was walking through the kitchen, I told Zach about my own experience in Washington. He stopped in his tracks and his head jerked my way. I might as well have claimed I'd won an Olympic gold medal. "When were *you* at the Capitol?" he asked. Though we are but a generation apart, he measures the chasm in geologic time. I often remind myself how old my father's friends looked to me when I was Zach's age. It helps me understand Zach's frame of reference. We all begrudgingly acknowledge, but never come close to understanding the import of, the lives our parents lived before we entered them. Not to mention the impact theirs are destined to have on our own.

My father, Nate Shore, Zach's grandfather, was forty-three years old when he rode a chartered bus from Pittsburgh to the nation's capital for Dr. Martin Luther King, Jr.'s March on Washington and his "I Have a Dream" speech. It was the only night of my childhood I can remember his being away from home. Nate's father, Israel Shorski, was even younger when as an insubordinate soldier in the czar's army he published an underground newspaper before fleeing for Ellis Island. In America he was a tailor and ran a corner grocery store. I don't remember my dad speaking of him much or at all. I can only surmise what his influence might have been.

Dad took his place with other political activists, union

leaders, and civil rights activists on the four-and-a-half-hour bus ride, stopping halfway at Breezewood for a meal and to use the bathroom. He was the assistant to Pittsburgh's congressman, and the trip was part of his job as well as a reflection of his beliefs. In my imagination I feel the dampness of the long, un-air-conditioned bus ride, hear songs and laughter from the back of the bus, and can see fruit and snacks being passed around.

In photos of the massive crowd at that historic event, taken from high above the steps of the Lincoln Memorial, it is virtually impossible to make out a face among the hundreds of thousands who attended. But taken together they form a uniquely American mosaic whose image is unforgettable. It took no special bravery on the part of my father to attend, but it did take conscience, commitment, and initiative. The power of the act was not, as is sometimes the case, in being the lone voice that speaks truth to power. It was just the opposite. It came from being one of too many to be counted, one of too many to be ignored. Our family and neighbors all felt part of something big, just by virtue of the fact that Dad went. Anonymous though he may have been in that large crowd, quiet and gentle as was his nature, we all felt he'd made his voice heard.

Five years later I got my turn. My parents bundled my sister and me into the backseat of their Chevy Impala and took us to the very same spot. It was 1968. Protests against the war in Vietnam were culminating in one of the biggest mass demonstrations ever—the Vietnam Moratorium. It was the subject of discussion in our high school social studies classes and of frequent debates at the local universities. Neighborhood churches and temples held teach-ins, and an abundance of alternative newspapers and magazines provided coverage. En route to Washington, I'm not sure whether I was against the war or just in favor of getting out of school for two days. En route back, I knew that at least part of my life's course had been set.

Unlike Zach, who was born in D.C. and takes its institutions and monuments for granted, it was all new and breathtaking to me, and left an indelible impression. The broad avenues. The white marble. The serenity surrounding our symbols of democracy. Pittsburgh knew nothing of public spaces. Even the corner hot dog vendors, which we did not have at home, impressed me.

I'd wake up early and sneak out of my parents' hotel suite, scouting the city, its staging areas, media encampments, and police formations. I'd bring back information about what was happening and whom I'd seen. Later, as we marched down Pennsylvania Avenue, I'd marvel at the photographers perched on streetlamps, the sweet harmony of the protesters' song "All We Are Saying Is Give Peace a Chance," and the variety of the buttons, banners, and posters.

My parents must have had some sense of the trip's value. Our family was not one that traveled often. We never once took a family vacation, a concept I wasn't aware of until years later, when I learned at college that other families did. In fact this was the only trip we ever made away from home. I don't think it was frugality so much as a lack of imagination and a certain contentment with everything we had.

So the very fact of the trip made a statement beyond that which my parents would have been able to make on their own. They weren't preachy, though they had definite and strong opinions, which I heard them voice at the dinner table and on the front porch on summer evenings. Both also modeled certain values, and they went out of their way to ensure that I was exposed to the collective conscience of which they were a part.

I was the only student from my class to make the trip. Our neighbors thought our family's behavior eccentric but harmless. Harmless it may have been, but not innocuous.

That trip was a formative experience. Most of the demonstrators were older than I, but not by much. I could see myself in their shoes down the road. I had been empowered, given a responsibility I could not ignore. The major issue of the day, the one that dominated headlines and led newscasts, was one that I was directly, though only very peripherally, engaged in. It was one that I could be engaged in. The decision was mine to make. Citizens could be a force in their government when they made themselves heard.

And now, finally, Zach was taking his own place on the Capitol grounds, within a hundred hours of the September 11 tragedy. It was not a protest, of course. Protest was out of fashion. The 1980s and '90s had seen protest marches dwindle in number and become captive to increasingly fringe and marginal groups. The natural corollary to peace and prosperity is complacency. There just hadn't seemed to be a lot to protest about. The very activity that once had been a badge of honor was now an occasion for ridicule.

Zach's participation in protesting had previously been reserved for burning issues like his curfew, how often he had to take a bath, and such oppressive inconveniences as having to use the computer to spell check his homework. He protested plenty, but within the four walls of his home. This was more a vigil, a show of support and national unity as well as sympathy toward the victims.

That's not to say he hadn't developed certain early instincts based on conscience. But they were more along the line of playground rules. Zach has always leapt to the defense of the underdog. He is quick to the rescue of a boy that others pick on. He identifies fiercely with Judaism and reacts strongly to anti-Semitism. The origins of such impulses are uncertain. I'd like to think it has something to do with his awareness of my work supporting hungry and homeless people. But it could just as well come from his ten years as a defenseman in hockey, where part of his job is protecting the goalie on his hockey team, who is sometimes hit unfairly after the referee's whistle. In the days after September 11 he seemed to have the same instinct for civilians hit unfairly while sitting at their desks in the World Trade Center. And thus Zach finds himself on the Capitol Mall. Making himself heard.

Until that day, understandably for a teenage boy, his world had not been much larger than the perimeter defined by school, home, and hockey rink. Sports trumped news. Rap music trumped reading. He'd been only marginally interested in the kinds of political affairs I've followed all my life, though I've sneaked some in where I could, the way you conceal a puppy's medicine in a bowlful of biscuit treats. I've smuggled news from the outside world into Zach's conscience the way contraband is smuggled into prisons.

By eleven o'clock that night, Zach was still not home from the Capitol. He'd only rarely been out this late, and almost never on his own or this far from his suburban Silver Spring, Maryland, home. Suddenly the world seems more dangerous than even Osama bin Laden can make it. One of Zach's classmates, J.P., is driving. J.P. is a good boy, but still just a boy, and my head is filled with terrifying statistics about teen driving and the increased danger every time the number of kids in a car increases. By a few minutes to midnight my anxiety is high. I channel surf and keep checking the clock. A second vigil has begun, right here in my own house.

My vigil is not just for Zach to get home safely. Though I pray for it, that is merely one leg of the journey whose safe passage I've watched over. No, my vigil has been maintained for a lot longer than one night. Mine has been the lifelong vigil nearly every parent keeps. It is not only for your child's safety, but for signs that your child is taking his or her own place in the world. That by the end of their journey through adolescence they are prepared to stand on their own. And that they will "do the right thing even when no one is watching."

To be vigilant is, literally, to watch over. A vigil means watching. Waiting. A young student observing where he fits in the larger order. Parents' sharp ears listening for the car to pull up. And listening to see if they have made themselves heard.

One weekend later in the year, Zach went to dinner with his girlfriend, Alison, and her parents. Zach and Alison had been dating for about six months, and the barrier to any contact with parents was cracking in a few places.

They took him to a nice Thai restaurant on Rockville Pike. For him this was a radical culinary departure. Absent the availability of pad Thai in a double-decker taco, I couldn't imagine what he was going to eat. Zach prefers his meals at the drive-thru window. Food just ain't food unless you can hold it in your hand. I was curious how he'd digest the combination of Thai food and his girlfriend's parents. When he got home I asked: "How was it, buddy?"

"Aw, it was okay. I didn't like it much but I found a few

things." After a pause he added, with an impossible combination of grimace and wan smile, "I took off my hat."

My eyes met his. We both understood the significance of the confession. We were silent for a moment as the import sank in. I wasn't sure which surprised me more, the deed itself or the generosity of his statement. For a moment I knew how Grant felt when Lee surrendered at Appomattox.

Zach has worn a baseball cap almost all of the time since he was five years old. It's his signature style and generally speaking not one I disapprove of. It became one way he defined his independence and sense of self. Resisting his parents is another way. The combination of resisting his parents in a matter related to his hat is most formidable.

Every time we've sat down at a restaurant for the past ten years, I've asked Zach to take off his hat. We've had this conversation just short of two thousand times. The mere suggestion seems to offend if not disgust him, as if some principle of intellectual integrity were at stake. In such circumstances he's a master of Socratic reasoning.

"Why?"

"Because you're in a restaurant."

"So what?"

"Nobody else has a hat on."

"I thought you told me it's not always right to do what everyone else does."

"That's true, but wearing a hat in a restaurant is just not polite."

"To who? I'll bet if you asked some of the other customers, they wouldn't care."

"Well, I care, Zach. It's just a matter of trying to teach you right from wrong. Please take it off."

"Do I have to?"

"I'd like you to. It's disrespectful."

"Why is it disrespectful?"

"Because it is," I say, realizing the trap I've created for myself. He might as well have yelled "Checkmate!" I'd fallen back on that last resort of parents and scoundrels. He realizes it too. The breach was large enough to fell the entire fortress.

"Yeah, that's what I thought."

Sometimes, depending on moods and circumstances, these conversations escalate wildly and at some cost to the evening. It's amazing how many times a parent loses control in trying to communicate the need for a child to control himself. At other times common sense would prevail on one side or the other. Of course Zach's hat didn't bother me personally the slightest bit. But since nature grants us foresight as compensation for otherwise growing feeble in mind and body, I had vaguely anticipated a day when he might sit down to dine with a girl he cared about, although even I hadn't anticipated Thai food or parents.

So for Zach to look me in the eye and volunteer, "I took off my hat," well . . . I kept my face a mask of indifference, but I wanted to do one of those little dances that a wide receiver does in the end zone just after he's scored a touchdown. Like a long simmering brew, a decade and a half of parenting suddenly reached the conversion point from futility to fruition.

My joy was tempered by the recognition of how pathetic it was to derive so much pleasure from so small a victory. I was like one of those kids who put five quarters into a vending machine to win a plastic charm worth five cents. Still, he had not only done the right thing, but he wanted me to know he'd done the right thing, and even more, there was an implied acknowledgment that I was the reason why. Parents get few such tributes—and most of them come at grave sites and hospital beds. They are disbursed sparingly while you are alive.

They say your conscience is what helps you do the right thing even if no one is watching. It takes years to develop, and the lesson I learned from Zach is not that kids will develop theirs eventually, but rather that kids will develop theirs if and only if their parents never relent in helping them.

There are no metrics for good parenting, no report cards. It's like a course you take pass-fail. You can assume you did well enough, but you're never really sure how well. And then one day, after years of chipping away at hard rock with what feels like a tiny ball-peen hammer, a shape begins to emerge, no longer rough and crude but almost suddenly smooth and beautiful.

I think I see Zach emerging. My hat's off to him.

. . .

After almost two decades of parenting, many of my ambitions for my children—the grades they'll make, the colleges they'll go into, the jobs they'll get—have fallen away like autumn leaves from a tree. As beautiful as they may be, they are secondary to what will really determine their quality of life. One ambition remains, one want that I have for them, which is for them to feel good about themselves. That one stands tall like a tree with deep roots, for with the right combination of self-esteem and inner peace there is little they will not be able to accomplish, few challenges that will come their way long after I'm gone that they won't be prepared to meet. If they can learn to navigate life by the beacon of conscience and have the confidence to abide it when it makes itself heard, they will live as fully and as richly as if I'd left them King Tut's treasure.

When Zach finally got home it was as if the energy of the entire crowd surged through him. "It was awesome, Dad. They asked us to lead the march. Everyone took our pictures: *Time, Newsweek,* they took like a hundred pictures of us. I'm sure we're gonna see them somewhere," he added, prophetically, and with eager anticipation.

Zach and his buddies drove to the Capitol propelled by a mix of reasons that included adventure, friendship, curiosity, independence, and some vague and undefined sense of the import of the moment. Some of it may have been a reflex. But they must also have had some sense that the world around them, what had always been the world of their parents, was becoming their world too, theirs to enjoy, to ruin, to defend. Most important of all came that sense that, photographed or not, there is a time to make oneself heard. In a democracy, one voice among many is still a powerful voice.

Two weeks later a meeting would be convened at Zach's school because a majority of the students had signed a petition requesting that the school fly the American flag. Waldorf had not flown one previously and no one had seemed to notice or care. Some thought it inappropriate for the Washington Waldorf School, as part of an international education movement, to fly the flag of just one country. But it could be that the flag was just too militaristic for some of these former veterans of the antiwar movement. The roles of parent and child had been completely reversed in the course of a generation. But the children felt strongly and persisted.

A conscience once awakened does not return to slumber. *The Christian Science Monitor* was right. It is "A Changed World." Not only around the globe but deep inside the conscience of those who decided, for the first time, to make themselves heard.

SMALLER WORLD, LARGER CONSEQUENCES

TODAY IS THE kind of gift that can't be bought, borrowed, ordered, or anticipated. It can't be any of these things because its qualities cannot be imagined in advance. I'm talking of course about the snow, all twenty-seven inches of it. Roads closed. Noise muffled. Snow is a most insistent enforcer of quiet, setting an example by the very silence of its descent.

I always marvel at the civilizing effect of snowfall. The many things we have to do—those many things we always do—we can't, and because we can't, it turns out that we don't really have to. And what we don't have to do, we don't have to think about. So other, less hurried thoughts get their chance to emerge, like a big old lumbering car that waits for a lull in speeding traffic to get on the freeway.

I am working by the large picture window that looks out on a backyard filled with trees. A few brave cardinals, sparrows, and squirrels are taking turns dive-bombing into the snow beneath the bird feeders, pecking for buried treasure. Gentle gusts push drifts against the chain-link fence until finally the fence disappears.

This sudden respite from routine is a chance to step back and account for the increased global relevance of acts of conscience. From al-Qaeda to military threats in Iran and

Korea to AIDS in southern Africa and famine in Ethiopia, world crises cascade upon one another, and it seems only a matter of time before the leaders we rely on to juggle them eventually let one drop.

Implicit in the argument that acts of conscience change the world is that people have an interest in changing and improving the world, not necessarily all of it, but at least the part of the world within their reach: their children's schools, the parks and streams they enjoy, the streets they live on. It assumes an appetite for change driven by self-interest rather than altruism, which is fine because altruism has its limits but self-interest rarely does.

But tending one's own backyard, however conscientiously, may no longer be enough. The fences we relied on to define and protect what is ours are no more relevant anymore than those that disappeared beneath the snow behind my house. Since September 11 we've learned that noxious weeds ten thousand miles away can overwhelm our most prized and protected seedlings. Technology, information, and communications have shrunk the globe to the point that no backyard is big enough or far enough from those who wish us ill.

"Think globally, act locally," the bumper stickers once proclaimed, as if establishing the perfect pragmatic balance. What a luxury that turned out to be. Confining activism to our immediate environs and expecting the rest of the world to benefit indirectly is as foolhardy as ignoring a bleeding foot because it happens to be at the far end of one's body.

If we've learned anything from the emotions unleashed after September 11, it is that our quality of life, whether in lower Manhattan or Broken Bow, Nebraska, is now inextricably linked to the quality of lives unknown, but no longer unknowable, half a world away.

Each of us now has a direct self-interest in the problems of far-off lands we once read about with detached intellectual curiosity: barriers to education and development in the Middle East and Persian Gulf, the eradication of poverty and disease in Africa, equal opportunity for women around the world. The international community's ability to address these problems today has a direct impact on tomorrow, not just at the United Nations or at the Agency for International Development, but in our ability to catch a plane without a two-hour wait, to feel safe enjoying a cup of coffee in a crowded Starbucks, to take our family on a vacation overseas, even to stroll carefree in the shadow of our own national monuments.

More than ever, changing *our* world requires changing *the* world. As with any challenge of this magnitude, government is not enough. No sooner has national service begun to be institutionalized, thanks to Presidents Clinton and Bush, than a call for international service must be imagined and sounded.

School systems must expand world history and foreign studies, as well as comparative religion and diverse exchange programs. Businesses must weigh short-term profits against the long-term costs of exploitation. The universal rationale of being "competitive" must be measured against our children's and grandchildren's vulnerability. We can't be exporters to the world without being citizens of the world. Failure to inspect our own values and conscience as global citizens will prove to be as dangerous as failing to inspect carry-on luggage.

For more than two days I've watched from my picture window as layer upon layer of white accumulates to demonstrate the enormous impact that can be had without making a single sound. Silence falls in layers too, and has its own power. Eventually it enables us to hear what very deep down we already know. We may not have invited the world into our backyard but it seems to have found its way. Gandhi said you must become the change you want to see in the world. Today the opposite is also true. We must help change the world if we are to become all we can be.

IX

Conscience Is a Lighthouse

Mankind's moral sense is not a strong beacon light, radiating outward to illuminate in sharp outline all that it touches. It is, rather, a small candle flame, casting vague and multiple shadows, flickering and sputtering in the strong winds of power and passion, greed and ideology. But brought close to the heart and cupped in one's hands, it dispels the darkness and warms the soul.

—JAMES Q. WILSON,
The Moral Sense

THE CONSENT OF THE GOVERNED

PARENTING, LIKE DEMOCRACY, requires the consent of the governed, and like democracy is easier when the governed are unaware of this inalienable right. Twist the arm of a politician or parent and they'll eventually confess their belief that knowledge in the wrong hands at the wrong time is a very dangerous thing.

When Zach and Mollie were quite young, they learned

through repetition. This is a polite way of saying they had to be told things many times before they ultimately listened. "Give your sister's bagel back to her . . . Give it back now . . . Do not eat any more of that . . . If I have to come over there . . ." And of course that old threat which damages parental credibility like a sledgehammer: "I'm not going to say it again." They couldn't be expected to learn any other way, and their progressive development was patience's own reward. Of course what seemed like patience then, in retrospect proved to be merely a light warm-up for the main event, a jog in the park compared to the grueling endurance of a marathon. The real test comes when they get older, because that's when they refuse to listen even though they understand every word as clear as a bell.

A young child's obedience fills a parent with prideful satisfaction. All of the hard work has paid off. You knew what you were doing after all.

This feeling changes as your child gets older. Because when your teenager listens and complies anywhere within the first five or ten times of being asked or told, you're as surprised and amazed as if the cat started doing card tricks.

But it is nature's genius that parents are not left bereft of all tools. Because just as the power to get one's children to listen diminishes, a compensating power increases in direct proportion. It is the power to mortify. When your children are anywhere between the ages of ten and twenty, you probably exercise this power so effortlessly that you may often not even be aware of it. It can be something as simple as popping in the wrong CD while your daughter's friends are in the car, or waiting at the curb too long to make sure your son's football teammate can get into his house. You don't even have to say anything. Sometimes just walking into the same room they are in can achieve the desired effect. Now that's power!

This is not a power that parents have to earn or that is dependent upon their skills, or even their relationships with their kids. It resides with all parents, and the only question is how it can be channeled and deployed most effectively.

I tested this power on a vacation with the children. The majesty of Half Dome isn't the only thing Zach and Mollie will remember from their week in Yosemite National Park. Rock climbing to the head of a waterfall, tubing on Bass Lake, the ferry over to Alcatraz were all new and special. But it was the flight home that had them riveted.

We were halfway back to Washington on a United Airlines 747 widebody when the pilot announced that the weather at Dulles Airport would be hot and humid compared to when we took off from cooler San Francisco. Mollie decided that she'd be more comfortable in shorts than jeans, so she reached into the carry-on bag stuffed under the seat in front of her and pulled out a pair of blue shorts. Like any girl her age, she looks for excuses to put on a new outfit. She was tucked into a window seat and didn't want to get out. Mollie is seventy-five pounds of agile arms and legs and has all the room she needs, even in an airline seat, to change clothes so discreetly that no one would be able to tell what she was doing.

When she finished, she hollered to me across the aisle. She had a huge smile and was gripping the edge of the blanket with one hand. "Dad, remember the jeans I was wearing when I got on the plane?" Her eyes widened in anticipation. "Well . . . ta daaa!" With that she pulled the blanket aside with one hand, waved her jeans at me with the other, and showed off the shorts she'd switched into.

"How did you do that?" I asked, exaggerating my shock.

She spread the blanket back across her lap and did a demonstration wiggle.

A plan took shape in my mind.

After a few minutes, Mollie resumed her preoccupation with her hand-held Game Boy computer, and when I was sure she wasn't looking I reached into my own bag and casually fished for a pair of my white Jockey shorts, which I retrieved and slipped into the left-hand pocket of the khakis I was wearing. I went back to reading my magazine. About thirty minutes later, a lifetime for a ten-year-old, I called over to Mollie, "Hey, Molls, watch this!"

I spread a blue airline blanket over my own lap, knowing that she had to be wondering what I could possibly be up to. Her brother was sitting in the row ahead of her and he looked over as well. Once I had the blanket covering me from the waist down, I reached my hands under it, bounced around a few times, shifted my weight, and then unbuckled my brown belt and pulled it off and waved it at Mollie. She gave me a look that said "Big deal," but I was just establishing the foundation for a grander illusion. When she saw I was not finished, her dismissive grin dissolved into a wide-eyed blend of confusion and concern.

Now I began my wriggling and squirming in earnest. Neither Zach nor Mollie could imagine what I was doing. They unlatched their seatbelts and leaned forward to get a better view. I struggled and grunted until I had their undivided attention. Then, after reaching into my pants pocket, I completed the illusion by pulling out the white Jockey shorts and waving them around my head like a caffeinated cowboy with his lasso.

Both kids recoiled in horror. They slammed their bodies into the backs of their seats and leaned away at an even greater angle than they had been leaning forward, pressing as close to the plane's windows as possible. Zach looked to see if other passengers were watching. Mollie covered her eyes with her hands.

Their lips could only form one word, and it was enunciated with genuine desperation: "Please." I was undeterred. I launched the Jockey shorts into orbit one more time. "Dad!" they shouted. *"Please."*

This parental ability to mortify is a potentially powerful tool, but probably more effective as a deterrent than for its first-strike capability. Still, parents need something at their disposal, for there comes a point where the role of parent approximates the ceremonial, like the Queen of England's, with authority to command but not compel. There must be times when the Queen finds this maddening. I imagine I have shared her frustration. Unfortunately, I have not maintained the same royal dignity.

One of the perverse dynamics in parent-child communications is that the more words you direct toward your child to elicit an acknowledgment of what is expected of him or her, the fewer words they use to respond. Offer a platter, get a crumb. Zach worked at this until he achieved a remarkable level of concision and economy. In fact, to the overwhelming majority of parental proclamations, he got his answer down to a crisp two words: "For you." As in, "One o'clock in the morning is kind of late to being going to bed, pal."

"For you," he'd say with a dismissive wave, and not look back.

"Academics have to come before football, Zach."

"For you."

"Zach, that is not an acceptable way to speak to your mother."

"For you," he'd reply with a steady gaze.

These two words came to have an unexpectedly violent effect on me.

"For any human being!" I would scream.

We hit bottom one hot Saturday afternoon when he was

asked to help with some yard work. Given the postage-stamp size of the fenced-in yard, there wasn't much to do in the first place: pull a few weeds, dig a couple of holes for the new shrubs, and untangle the hose. It was twenty minutes of work, and the only downside was that it would reduce his TV watching to a mere five and a half hours that afternoon. Still, somehow the very request offended deeply. Only an Orthodox Jew (which he is not) celebrating the Sabbath could have been offended more deeply. For about twenty minutes he did as little as possible, demonstrating the opposite of multitasking, completing one chore and instantly retiring inside the air-conditioned house. I'd call him out again and the negotiation would begin anew, both of us a bit more frustrated than before.

As Zach and I faced off, debating his First Amendment right to express such an opinion, the yard work soon became irrelevant, a mere proxy battle for control of the entire household. As in Vietnam or Cuba or Angola, the practical value was insignificant, but the strategic stakes were enormous. At least that's the way I perceived it at the time. If the domino theory applied anywhere, it was here. If he didn't listen now, he wouldn't listen the next time, or the next time; in fact, he might never listen again. I drew a line in the sand, and together we entered the quagmire.

Before the first "How dare you . . ." had left my lips, Zach brushed past me. With nothing there to absorb or reflect my words, they drifted limply away. Zach turned toward the house and I knew he would go to his room. By the time I reached his room, I had only a few options and none of them were good.

I'm happy to say we haven't had many incidents like that. But I'll never forget the moment when I looked into his eyes and realized that he was of an age and size that I couldn't make him do something he didn't want to do, and he looked into mine and saw that I had realized it. From that point on it would become more a question of what his conscience told him, and whether or not he listened to it, whether or not he and I had built up a large enough reservoir of respect, trust, and love to draw upon at times like these.

TO THE LIGHTHOUSE

AS WE CHECK out of the Regency Hotel in New York, Zach turns to me and says: "I like this place because they called me 'sir' . . . without adding 'you're making a scene.'" We're standing at the curb on Park Avenue, waiting for our car to be brought up amid a sea of taxis, and I'm staring at him, surprised by his brand of humor. "It's from *The Simpsons,*" he finally admits, which I should have guessed, because the show is the source of much of his conversational English. Nevertheless, it fits the moment as we end another phase of a vacation which included *The Lion King,* F.A.O. Schwarz, long walks through Central Park, and a day at Ellis Island.

A week together in the close quarters of car and hotel

room was also an opportunity to foster certain appreciations within the kids. Or at least to make the attempt. Some were mundane, like getting Zach to tuck in his shirt at dinner each night. He opposed this with the same vehemence with which a previous generation opposed the war in Vietnam. Or persuading Mollie that if everyone else on the beach could hear 'N Sync through her headphones, then the volume was too high. Others were more profound, like tracing Grandpa Shorski's steps through Ellis Island and trying to convey a sense of the privileges and responsibilities bequeathed us by brave ancestors—what Mark Helprin in his novella *Ellis Island* expressed by saying, "To give to another without reward is the only way to compensate for our own mortality, and perhaps the binding principle of this world."

There is much more to recall from our visit—the mile-high pastrami sandwiches at the Carnegie Deli, the hour-long backup at the Holland Tunnel, visiting the set of *Saturday Night Live*. But Mollie will likely remember the trip as her journal captured it:

> We are about a hour into the ride when my dad starts telling us we have to stay with each other because in New York people get drunk and throw bricks at each other and might steel [*sic*] you if you don't stay close. Well right then I was very confused and thought "Then why are we coming here for a family vacation?" I also realized it is going to be great! My dad had arranged the trip so that we spend 2 days in the

city and then we will go to Montauk in this hotel that is so beautiful!

Montauk *is* beautiful. We spent four days on the wide white beaches backed by dunes and cliffs. Zach and Mollie love it for different reasons. Mollie is on a mission, and that mission is to get a tan. But an eleven-year-old has only a beginner's understanding of how that works. Lying on a blanket in her two-piece yellow Speedo for just shy of three minutes, she hollers down to where Zach and I are playing catch near the cold foamy surf:

"Dad, am I tan yet?"

"We just got here, Molls."

"How long does it take?"

"More than three minutes, hon."

"I think it's too cool to get a tan." The sky is deep blue and the sun's warmth is in the eighties, but the ocean breeze has deceived her.

"Oh, you'll definitely get a tan. It's hot enough. It just doesn't feel that way 'cause we're near the water."

"How long?"

"It won't work if you keep asking," I warn.

Zach walks over to investigate, impatient upon learning that the rationale for being interrupted is a discussion of tanning. He hopes to play baseball for his new high school, so we take our mitts everywhere we go. Watching him at water's edge, nearing six feet tall and fielding fly balls with ease as a continent stretches out behind his lean but muscular body, I see him as Atlas astride the globe.

The rhythm of our game—the bending and stretching, catching and throwing, following the long arc of a white ball across azure sky—is pure therapy. The sand is soft and not easy to run across. I notice, after half an hour, that my throws are growing weaker and shorter, but his keep getting stronger. The same physical exertion that depletes me energizes him. Within him may lie the secret to perpetual motion.

Fifteen minutes more and my rotator cuff begins to burn. Fortunately Zach is ready to swim. I call to his sister.

"Hey, Molls. Zach and I are going in the water. Come with us."

"Am I tan yet?" She lifts her head, chin to her chest, and surveys her body, but the sun makes it too bright to tell.

"You're getting there."

"But I won't get a tan if I move around."

"That's not true, sweetie."

"I have to lay perfectly still."

I try to explain that the water can magnify the sun's rays for an even stronger tan, but she dismisses this as some kind of crude parental trick. Moments later, I see her peek under the shoulder strap of her bathing suit in search of a tan line. Finding none, she lies even more still, like a soldier at rigid attention.

Zach loves the ocean and can stay in it for hours on end. A thunderstorm the previous evening has roiled the waters, and the waves crest between six and ten feet before thrashing onto shore. Zach rises on top of their swell or dives under them. He is afraid to ride them in (thankfully) but he doesn't mind planting his feet in the sand and taking all but their strongest blows. Many times he buckles as a wave buries him. He disappears momentarily from view, then comes up shaking water from his face like a puppy. The bracing physical contact is something he not only enjoys, but needs, just as he needs to check and be checked in hockey, just as he needs to wrestle his dad in the living room so many nights after work. Collisions are caresses to Zach.

This makes the ocean a perfect playmate. It does not tire like a middle-aged father. It doesn't quit at dinnertime. It is not provoked by Zach's shouts, taunts, or threats. Most important, it is stronger than this strong boy of fifteen. He can't break it or hurt it. The waves are enormous and it is too deep to stand where they break. The only safe way back to shore is to let the current carry you, in softer diagonals, about fifty yards down the coast.

I don't get cold, just exhausted. When I'm satisfied I've been in the water three times longer than any other parent, I turn to go. *"Aw, c'mon,"* he bellows in protest. *Enough* is a word Zach hasn't learned and doesn't want to. "Just three more, Dad. . . . That doesn't count as one of the three. . . . Okay, one for good luck, just one. . . ." His entreaties are persuasive. There can't be many summers left when he'll want to play with me this way. It's only as we're finally leaving, another twenty minutes later, that we notice the two large red flags planted on either side of the empty lifeguard chair signaling that the beach is closed due to dangerous riptides.

We find a seafood shack by the side of the road for lunch, and then we drive the six miles east to Montauk Point to see the first lighthouse in New York State. It's my idea, which of course makes it suspect. Mollie is amenable, but Zach registers a protest faster than a game-show contestant pounds the buzzer. A lighthouse is too inanimate an object for him. His contempt for something so "boring" is palpable. Only when told that he can climb the 137 iron steps to the top does his attitude change.

The lighthouse was originally situated three hundred feet from the edge of a bluff called Turtle Hill. The early planners understood erosion and accurately calculated losing a foot a year. Two hundred years later, two hundred feet of that bluff has been claimed by the sea. Now fully automated, the lighthouse is maintained by the U.S. Coast Guard and continues to aid navigation, visible for nineteen miles. Day and night it stands like a lone and loyal sentry.

The 110-foot tower is of whitewashed sandstone with a broad band of brown painted around the middle. Its walls are six feet thick at the base. Behind it squats the keeper's dwelling. Originally only one keeper was required to maintain the lighthouse, but few jobs ever required such devotion and dedication to duty. The keeper lit the lamps at dusk and extinguished them at dawn. This also entailed hauling fuel up the tower, keeping the oil reservoir full, trimming the wicks of a dozen or more oil lamps, and keeping the lantern glass and reflectors clean, as well as constant polishing of brass and painting of walls exposed to harsh elements. Newer lenses, though, required continual attendance throughout the night, and two assistant keepers were brought on to share the watch and the expanded house. Their conscientious vigilance was all that stood between safe passage and disaster at sea.

Montauk's lighthouse is the fourth oldest in the United States, authorized by the Second Congress under President George Washington in 1792. Its purpose was to serve as a landfall light for ships bound from Europe to New York, as well as to guide coastal navigation to ports in Connecticut, Rhode Island, and Massachusetts. Constructing a lighthouse that would benefit the commerce of multiple states was a logical priority for the new federal government.

But I didn't bring the kids here for a history or economics lesson. I want them to see the lighthouse for its stark beauty and because it says something about steadfastness, duty, and commitment. Standing at its base and looking up at its tower with one hand shielding my eyes from the bright sun, I think of the cathedrals I've gazed up at, though of course the contrast is striking. The architecture of a lighthouse is spare and exceedingly simple. This is no place for the ornate. Construction takes months or years, not the decades and centuries the great cathedrals required. Its purpose is not varied, but singular; it serves not the many, but the few. Instead of stained glass windows that admit a flood of light, it projects one powerful and sweeping beam that briefly slices the darkness and moves on.

I can't fail to view a lighthouse as like one's conscience. It's always there, an insistent reminder of important truths. But whether we allow its light to guide us is something different entirely. The choice is ours to make or reject.

The lighthouse at Montauk flashes its powerful light every five seconds. By day the tower itself serves as a landmark by which mariners navigate. The value of a lighthouse to a sailor is that it is a fixed point, the one constant in a seascape being reshaped relentlessly by changing winds and weather. To ignore it is to drift perilously close to rocky shoals. And so it is with our conscience.

Hundreds of lighthouses dot our coasts from the Outer Banks of North Carolina to the over 3,500 craggy miles of Maine's shoreline, from the length of California to Oregon's rugged coast. They were the first order of business for our young government, and they remain among the oldest structures on the American continent. Time and tides may erode their foundations but can never diminish the need for the protection they offer.

The life of a lighthouse keeper, cold, wind-whipped, and

often isolated, could be monotonous and lonely. The job required equal parts conscience and faith. For although his light is visible to ships at sea for miles around, the ships are not often visible to him. Just as leaders can never be sure who their followers will be, who will see and respond to whatever light radiates from their actions, so the lighthouse keeper must have faith that conscience has its sure rewards.

"People get what lighthouses are about," says Peter Ralston, who founded Maine's Island Institute to protect the natural and cultural heritage of the state's island communities. "Lighthouses speak to vigilance. They speak to caring. They speak to being there. They speak to helping other human beings."

KEEPING YOUR CONSCIENCE STRONG AND FIT

IN JUNE of 2003 I went to Exeter as the graduation speaker for City Year's New Hampshire Corps. It was a carbon copy of the nearly dozen City Year graduations I've attended: corps members charging down the center aisle, calisthenics, Moccasin awards to corporate supporters, a slide show set to inspirational music. That didn't diminish the power of young leaders marking a rite of passage in which they and their families had good reason to celebrate and take pride.

The twenty-one corps members in khakis and red jackets (despite the heat) were eloquent, energetic, and disciplined; diverse in style, united in purpose. Some of the guys had buzz cuts and others had long, unruly hair. Some of the girls giggled or cried, and some spoke with the poise of women twice their age. They all evangelized idealism with the passion of converts, giving testimony to the idea that one person can make a difference. There was fierceness to their convictions and I found poignancy in knowing they are destined to soften with age as surely as once well-toned abs.

I was a stranger to most of them. The first time I spoke at a City Year event, more than a decade ago, was as a mentor a few years ahead of the corps. Today I represent a different and distant generation. It is easy to succumb to the notion that those of us older and more experienced are the ones with something to teach and that the young graduates before us are the ones with something to learn. But "older and more experienced" can also mean more experienced at compromise, accommodation, and moral relativism. Unsure of what I could contribute, I was more certain of what I might take away.

I wanted to make the point that changing the world doesn't always require money, fame, political power, or even fully funded national service. Sometimes the slightest personal gesture creates the greatest public ripple. I told the story about Pee Wee Reese's hand on Jackie Robinson's shoulder during those ugly first days of integrated baseball.

I knew at least some of them would be looking for guidance, something that says if you want to live a life of conscience, here is how to do it. I had no such formula to offer. Matters of conscience are uniquely personal. Each of us must find the way that is authentically our own.

From the lectern, I could stare into their eyes and see both innocence and skepticism, each struggling with the other to prevail and, in the process, creating a potent mix. Most of the corps members are between nineteen and twenty-three, an age at which young people can fall into confusion and anger. Resentment of what is unfair or unjust is visceral, raw, and unchecked, unlike the older and paler shade that is intellectual, balanced, and guarded. The hypocrisy that typically disguises and protects injustice is instantly detected, disdained, and dismissed. My goal was not to talk about my life's lessons but to help them hold on to theirs.

What I tried to convey was this: Many times we are witness to the unfair or unjust, maybe even the outrageous. City Year founder Alan Khazei says everyone has a "justice nerve." Once it is struck you are not the same. But from the time we are children, we are warned that it's not enough to get angry; you need to do something about it, take constructive action. I wanted the corps to see that the converse is also true. It is not enough to just do something. You must also get and stay angry. Or incensed. Or impassioned. Organizing, fundraising, advocacy, and service are not enough. It is not motion but *e*motion that drives the work of change. Without it, the wheels will spin and the horn may blare, but you'll lack the traction to move forward.

Acts of conscience can change the world, but they don't happen by accident. Nor can they always be planned. But they can be prepared for. The best you can do is keep your conscience finely tuned, as a pitcher does his arm or a batter his swing. A conscience needs exercise, just like our heart, lungs, biceps, and quads. The best workout is to put it in those positions that served as the catalyst for your efforts in the first place, to expose it not just to service but to those who desperately need to be served and may never be. That powerful connection to self and soul, to the "still small voice within," is what's behind every act of conscience from Jan Karski's bravery in exposing the Holocaust to Dorothea Lange's photos of migrant poverty.

That is about as prescriptive as I can get. But the absence of a set and simple answer, of an arrow pointing the way, does not mean there are not some common questions to ask, questions that guide the way like lanterns bordering a rocky path. Questions such as: "What course would I choose if I were personally immune from the consequences?" or "Am I making the same choice I would advise my child to make?" or "Will this decision look as right twenty years from now as it does now?"

Such questions can be heavy lifting, and as in any workout they require many reps. But the result will be a stronger, fitter conscience, one that will require no strain to use, and will be ready to go when you need it.

THE LIGHTHOUSE AT GOOSE ROCKS

AT THE MOUTH of the Kennebec River lies the small town of Cape Porpoise. It is built around a sheltered harbor that supports a small but busy fishing industry. Cape Porpoise is the supply depot for Goose Rocks Beach. When residents of Goose Rocks need a hot meal, a fresh lobster, or anything at all during the ten months each year that their general store is closed, they come to Cape Porpoise. It is not even a ten-minute drive to the whitewashed, gray-roofed buildings of the Wayfarer Restaurant, the Captain's Table, and Bradbury Bros. grocery store with its post office, videos, and surprisingly good selection of wines from around the world.

Like Goose Rocks, everything about Cape Porpoise exudes the relaxed, carefree attitude of a summer vacation idyll. Leisure is the town's business. Its denizens adhere to a strict schedule of morning sails, afternoon naps, and ice cream cones at sunset. There is one exception. Cape Porpoise hosts one sentry always at work, always on watch. It is a responsibility born of geography, and thus entirely inescapable. It is a small lighthouse called Goat Island Light. It is the light I see flicker, across the water, from my window at Goose Rocks Beach.

Looking east from the Cape Porpoise harbor, past the rocking, faded fishing boats stacked with lobster traps, one's eyes fall first upon a tiny scrap of island, no greater in length than a suburban strip mall. Green at its center and surrounded by a hardscrabble rocky fringe like the stubble on an old sailor's chin, this is Goat Island. The tuft of land rising above the blue ocean is so small that it already holds the maximum of what can be built upon it: a squat lighthouse, a home, a boathouse, and an oil house.

At low tide, you can reach Goat Island from the Cape Porpoise harbor by walking across mudflats where men in high rubber boots dig for clams. At night, from any house on Goose Rocks Beach, one can look across the bay and see, every few seconds—every six, to be exact—the twinkle-flash at the horizon that is Goat Island Light. It is a pale light and slight, its consistency its great and undeniable virtue. At first you must focus and search to locate it. But the reward is that once you know where to look, it will never leave you.

Goat Island Light is one of sixty-six lighthouses that mark the Maine coastline, one of the more than eight hundred lighthouses that protect the entire U.S. coast and Great Lakes shores.

The message it flashes is common to every lighthouse: "Beware the danger marked by my light. Safety lies in staying your course."

Many lighthouses, constructed of massive stone blocks, tower a hundred feet and more into the sky. Goat Island Light is a modest affair as lighthouses go: a twenty-five-foot brick tower painted bright white, built in the 1880s to replace a structure first erected in 1834. Dangerous rocks near Goat

Island claimed forty-six vessels between 1865 and 1920, with the keepers at Goat Island often rushing into rough seas to pick up survivors. Today a modern 300 mm optic lens enables the lighthouse to be an active aid to navigation.

From a distance the diminutive Goat Island Light lacks the appearance of strength and majesty that so many great lighthouses project. It is not built high on a forbidding cliff, nor rising out of roiling waters. Its light is no more elevated than a third-story bedroom. It requires no craning of the neck to take in. No ribbon of red makes it stylish. If Maine's collective personality is taciturn, modest, practical, and unassuming, then this lighthouse makes a perfect houseguest.

The keeper's dwelling on Goat Island, just a few steps from the lighthouse, looks like one of those plastic Monopoly hotels, square and squat with a sloping red roof. From across the harbor it looks small enough to pinch between finger and thumb and plunk down somewhere else. Although in 1990 Goat Island Light became the next to last lighthouse in the United States to be automated (Boston Light was last in 1998), the nearby towns of Biddeford and Kennebunkport felt that having a keeper on Goat Island was important to protect the island and lighthouse station from vandalism, so the dwelling continues to be occupied.

For most of us, lighthouses are admired and enjoyed, but not necessarily used for the purpose for which they were built. Only a tiny handful of mariners actually avail themselves of lighthouses in navigation. Yet lighthouses have a powerful draw upon the rest of us. They are tourist destinations. They hold our gaze. Lighthouse calendars and postcards proliferate, along with paperweights and a wide variety of souvenir replicas. This attraction and appeal might tell us something about who we are, and even more about who we want to be.

An expert on lighthouses I am not. Beyond visiting several while vacationing, researching some of their history, and reading accounts of the lives of the lighthouse keepers, my knowledge is neither advanced nor highly specialized. But what I lack in expertise I've sought to compensate for in reflection. I have spent many quiet hours in the early morning and in the dead of the night alone at a window staring at Goat Island Light.

More often than not, my identification with lighthouses has come as a parent. What parent would not like to see himself as an unwavering and dependable beacon for his children? But the metaphor is double-edged. Like the lighthouse that never ceases to warn of danger, yet receives not so much as an acknowledgment that the warning has been understood, or even received, a parent can shine the light on rocky shores but cannot ensure that the child will steer clear of them.

I talk to my children constantly about school, driving, alcohol, tobacco, sex, friendship, character, service—the same issues on which most parents seek to provide guidance. There are many times when you want to warn your child stridently but, having made your point, have no choice but to stand mute. And when you are lucky enough to see your children sail on safely, don't expect them to wave in gratitude as they go by.

So maybe when they look at a lighthouse, Zach and Mollie will see for themselves something that would not have been effective for me to say: that strength brings responsibility, that duty requires conscience, and that life can change forever in the blink of a light. Maybe that white tower rising above an ocean of blue can demonstrate what a parent strives to convey: that the moment you feel most alone may be when you're having the greatest impact. And that as the tides pull and the world turns and the waves crash, there is no greater power than the beacon that sets a true course.

ACKNOWLEDGMENTS

First I'd like to round up and thank the usual suspects who play such a critical role in helping my books come into being. Their talent, generosity, and friendship are anything but usual: my editor, Jon Karp; my agent, Flip Brophy; my sister, Debbie Shore; and my colleague Chuck Scofield. With eyes, ears, and instincts that are second to none, they are the finest friends and colleagues an author could have.

For even more unusual sources of support and sustenance, I am grateful to Rosemary Jordano, Leah Steinberg, and Jeff Swartz, who were there when the light shined but also when it flickered. Intimates all, what they've taught me about connecting head and heart could fill a book of its own. Rosemary especially sought to make every page the best it could be, a standard embodied in her work and life, one which will, hopefully, over the course of our life together, rub off on me.

I'm indebted to the mentors, friends, and colleagues who helped research, provide, or review material for me: Joel Fleishman, Ashley Graham, Andy Hastings, Evan Hochberg,

Will Kanteres, Alan Khazei, Danny Meyer, Mario Morino, Lowell Weiss, Scott Wilkerson, and Nina Zolt.

Finally, a hearfelt thanks to each and every member of the staffs of both Share Our Strength and Community Wealth Ventures, whose compassion, capabilities, and commitment I am grateful for every day.

PHOTO: © RALPH ALSWANG

BILL SHORE is the founder and executive director of Share Our Strength, a national nonprofit organization that has raised more than $150 million to support antihunger and antipoverty organizations worldwide since its founding in 1984 and has mobilized tens of thousands of individuals to contribute their talents to its efforts. Shore is also chairman of Community Wealth Ventures, Inc., a subsidiary of Share Our Strength, which provides strategic counsel to corporations, foundations, and nonprofit organizations interested in creating community wealth. He is the author of *Revolution of the Heart* and *The Cathedral Within*. He lives outside Washington, D.C., and can be reached via e-mail at bshore@strength.org.

ABOUT THE TYPE

This book was set in Weiss, a typeface designed by a German artist, Emil Rudolf Weiss (1875–1942). The designs of the roman and italic were completed in 1928 and 1931 respectively. The Weiss types are rich, well-balanced, and even in color, and they reflect the subtle skill of a fine calligrapher.